Helena

I hope you enjoy the

David Guillebaud

ADVANCE PRAISE

"David Guillebaud's book is a wake-up call for boards and executive teams. He presents powerful evidence of the game-changing challenges disruption across all industries presents. He's spot on in his assertion that many companies are paralyzed by the paradox it has created. Their legacy environment is killing them in the long-term, but keeping them alive in the short-term – how do organizations transform themselves? This book first boldly challenges business leaders to accept the seriousness of this situation. David then offers practical advice on how to reinvent the business model by using the best of the legacy, and integrate that with the new. A must read for all existing and aspiring leaders."

Stephen Newton, Managing Partner, Elixirr LLP

"David Guillebaud has been a leading voice over many years on how the internet and related technologies will disrupt and transform the airline industry. Much of what he was saying 20 years ago has proved to be true. His highly readable book gives an excellent summary of the forces of digital and organizational disruption, and challenges management to get out of a state of denial and get ready with survival strategies."

Alex Cruz, Chairman and CEO, British Airways

"This is an important book. Twenty years after Clayton Christensen's revelation that managers can do everything right and yet succumb to a disruptor, disruption remains a hot topic, largely because so little has been done about it. The author attributes this convincingly to managerial denial and sets out how this can and must be addressed, with solutions ranging from the creation and spin-off of potentially disruptive ventures to building a 'digital age disruptive' organization.
The book sparkles. Guillebaud possesses an intellectually curious, wry and subtly iconoclastic mind and this, along with his diverse and fascinating hinterland, makes his writing as original and stimulating as any to be found in business literature. His examples, anecdotes and metaphors range well beyond the obvious – the Dells, easyjets and Ubers – and even touch the sublime, from Taoist managerial theory and African Big Man leadership style to the micromalthus, a bug which devours its own mother! Read, admire, be inspired."

Vaughan Evans, Business Strategist and author, *Key Strategy Tools: The 80+ Tools for Every Manager to Build a Winning Strategy*

"The enterprise world is undergoing fundamental transformation –
and David Guillebaud understands how and why it's happening and
what to do about it. In this book he shows that the disruptive forces
now at work – accelerating technology, wired consumers, changing
organizational structures and evolving workplace relationships – are all
sources of potential advantage for companies and leaders who are ready
to take them seriously. Drawing on a body of hard-won human insights
that we both share, David outlines a practice that can lead us from a
state of denial toward the mastery of our present complexities."

Theodore Taptiklis, Co-founder, The Human Methods Lab, author of
Unmanaging: Opening up the Organization to its Own Unspoken Knowledge

"Disruption denial is a topic close to the centre of what people at the
top of big enterprises struggle with and have struggled with for many
years. The core of the issue is exactly what David Guillebaud identifies
in this timely book – how to keep the business model that makes
the money turning efficiently while also shifting and adapting it to
the changing business environment. There are no easy answers, but
Guillebaud gives some useful pointers. And persistence can pay off –
for example, Jeff Immelt seems to be pulling this off at GE after a
protracted period of recovery from the implosion of GE Capital.
A stimulating and enjoyable read for any executive wanting
to confront disruption challenges seriously."

Nick Fell, Marketing Director, SAB Miller

"Over many years, David Guillebaud has been challenging CEOs to
rethink their business models and organizations to make them fit for
purpose in a world of accelerating change and disruption. His book is
essential reading for managers who want an easily digestible synthesis
of the forces of technological and organizational disruption, as well
a challenging read about why it is that many established companies
underestimate or chose to ignore the potential threats and opportunities.
He also gives his readers a practical framework of things companies must
do to get out of denial and a road map for survival in the disrupted
world. Sobering but important food for thought for all companies!"

Julian Drinkall, CEO, Alpha Plus, former President, EMEA
Cengage Learning, CEO Macmillan Education

"This is an important book and a challenge to established institutions to "get real" about the scale and pace of disruption. David Guillebaud's chatty book blends deep analysis with personal anecdotes, and makes this vast topic easily digestible. His thesis that established organizations are in a state of denial and trapped in the status quo is sobering, but his suggestions about what to do about it are encouraging. Easy to read, this book gives very good solutions to managers who are confronted by the usual problem of older middle management blocking disruptive initiatives coming from their younger fellows."

Francois Heriard-Dubreuil, Chairman, Remy Cointreau and Fondation INSEAD

"It doesn't matter what side of 'the pond' you live on or what your company does ... disruption is coming to you and you cannot avoid it. David Guillebaud's book, Disruption Denial, is not a book for my 'to read' list ... it's top on my TO DO list. He is right as he has been for so many years as a senior confidant and consultant to many of the world's best-known companies and leaders. We all know that disruption is an ever-present reality but what David has done is laid out a framework for what we can do to prepare for it and thrive with each new wave of change. Each year brings an increasing rate of change and challenge yet there are immense opportunities with each challenge. One of my most disruptive companies in the medical field is a living example of how to capitalize on the very principles that David has clearly laid out. He is right and it's wise to listen...especially when you have the ability to act on it. Don't just read his book...do what he says; you'll be the better for it."

Flip Flippen, Founder and Chairman, Flippen Group

"David Guillebaud has identified a major challenge for established businesses which is not that they don't recognize emergent threats but that they are often unable to overcome their own culture to do anything to really respond. Leaders should read his advice on how to energize their businesses to meet the new disruptors."

Sir Ian Cheshire, Chairman, Debenhams, former CEO Kingfisher

Disruption Denial is an exceptional book sweeping into the commercial, managerial and psychological heart of a business world in turmoil. David Guillebaud opens a refreshingly new window on the opportunity, indeed necessity, which so many businesses and their leaders have before them to prosper amid forces of disruption. Conventional wisdom is turned on its head…This is a call to arms, which, while never underplaying the tough realities of making organisations better, is fundamentally optimistic. This optimism is founded on faith in people who have the potential to set aside conventional constraints and follow a refreshed vision."

Stephen Warrington (from the Foreword) Business advisor and Board Director, previously partner at McKinsey, Diamond and PwC and Group Strategy Director at Barclays Group

"In this new book, David Guillebaud shows change-reluctant organizations and denial-plagued managers how to understand and take advantage of the seemingly existential threats of technological development, information ubiquity, organizational inadequacy and growing consumer power. He writes with the credibility and lucidity that come from many years of experience in helping senior managers confront and overcome their worst fears. Far from being preachy or patronizing, he speaks directly to the reader, using many real-world and recognizable examples to illustrate his points. If you only have time to read one book on management this year, choose this one."

Christopher (Rusty) Tunnard, Professor of International Business, The Fletcher School, Tufts University

"At last, the inertia of big clients is revealed, invaluable insight for getting to grips with dealing with big companies! My tech operations company boasts many such giant corporations as clients and David Guillebaud's book gives real insight in how they do business - and provides an invaluable "behind the scenes" insight of the struggles they face in confronting fundamental change. If you like me are growing a business which reinvents something they need, Disruption Denial provides insider knowledge which you can use to your advantage in pitching your services. Read it, you will enjoy it!"

Rich Coles, Founder and CEO of trafficRich

Published by
LID Publishing Limited
One Adam Street, London WC2N 6LE

31 West 34th Street, 8th Floor, Suite 8004,
New York, NY 10001, U.S.

info@lidpublishing.com
www.lidpublishing.com

A member of:

BPR Business Publishers Roundtable

www.businesspublishersroundtable.com

Printed in Great Britain by TJ International
ISBN: 978-1-910649-77-0

Cover and page design: Caroline Li

DIS RUPTION
DENIAL

WHY COMPANIES ARE IGNORING THE DISRUPTIVE
THREATS THAT ARE STARING THEM IN THE FACE

DAVID GUILLEBAUD

LONDON   MONTERREY
MADRID   SHANGHAI
MEXICO CITY   BOGOTA
NEW YORK   BUENOS AIRES
BARCELONA   SAN FRANCISCO

CONTENTS

ACKNOWLEDGEMENTS

This book has turned out to be a synthesis, even apotheosis, of the experiences of my whole working life. There have been so many influences that it is difficult to acknowledge them all.

For example, Frank Davis was my first boss at Esso; he gave me belief in myself and space to express contrarian views. Leslie Pincott was managing director at Esso when I was his assistant in my mid-20s – thank you, Leslie, for taking me seriously! Phillip Hawley taught me to hire people who were better than me. Rusty Tunnard inspired me to see a digital future in a meaningful way before this became commonplace. Lawrence Hunt thought I could help him grow a software business and a dot-com start-up when I thought I had little to contribute. Stephen Warrington showed me that you can build a successful business with a human face. Thank you all.

Tim Jones fired off the spark that ignited the fire to get me going on this book. He listened carefully to my rantings as we waited to catch planes and reassured me that I had something important and original to say. Other INSEAD friends, Francois Heriard-Dubreuil and Henk van Wijk, added their encouragement for me to get started. Without their nudging, encouragement and feedback, I would not have persevered.

Scott Bauer and Eoin O'Gorman got me involved in the digital disruption arena. Many thanks for listening as we crafted appropriate solutions for my business friends who needed their help.

I would like to highlight the special contributions of Theodore (Ted) Taptiklis and David Mullins to the content of this book.

While I got to know Ted at INSEAD, his important insight that organizations were the problem, not the solution, to business performance chimed strongly with me 20 years later. I have remained a cheerleader for his important work with Storymaker and the Human Methods Lab ever since, and he has contributed greatly to my attempts to marry his reality with mine. The denial by enterprises of the nature, scope, scale and immediacy of threatening change has fascinated me throughout my career and Ted has given me the perspective to better understand this. At one time we were going to write a book together but we never quite got round to it; much of the latent content has probably found its way into this tome!

Professor John Shotter spent agreeable hours with me providing me with a basis in psychology, family therapy and philosophy for better understanding the phenomenon of dysfunctional behaviours in the workplace. I am grateful for his patience!

David Mullins came into my life much more recently, but his input has been no less important. He has provided the intellectual heft to the wrestling match we have been conducting about business models and platforms. I have learned so much from David, and if there is useful stuff in this book for senior executives in seeing a practical way forward for moving toward platforms from legacy, it is due to him. He has a mighty brain encompassing a whole range of academic disciplines – there is never a dull moment with David! I have seen him in action, and he is an amazing combination of creative mind, pragmatic business partner and reliable friend to harassed senior executives.

I am grateful to my other friends and colleagues at Elixirr, and particularly Stephen Newton, Brandon Bichler and Brian Kalms, for their encouragement and practical support in the journey of this book. I have much enjoyed my association with the firm, and we share a common fascination with preparing today's firms for the disruptive realities of tomorrow. Thanks to Katie Gillett for giving me helpful feedback on generational tribes of consumers.

Special mention must be made to Oli Freestone. I am particularly indebted to Oli for the invaluable role he played in beating this book into shape, for his helpful criticism and wise counsel, not to mention his attention to detail in getting the book ready for the publisher. Thank you to baby Joseph for giving him the space to do this important work!

As an experienced, published author, Vaughan Evans helped me believe that my book might even get published! He forced me to sharpen up my criticism of the shareholder capitalistic model of the enterprise being a root cause of corporate denial. He contributed strongly to the definition of the "traps" that senior executives find themselves in.

I mention and quote from the published work of many learned authors throughout his book, and their contributions are acknowledged with grateful thanks. I must make special mention of the work of Frederic Laloux and Sangeet Choudary, both of whom gave me genuine "aha!" moments when I discovered their work. I am hoping to develop close relationships with both of these gentlemen in the future.

Laloux's book, *Reinventing Organizations*, really excited me – for the first time someone had studied real companies that had been adopting the kind of organizational practices I had been banging on about for so long. Choudary's book, *Platform Scale*, lifted the scales from my eyes so I could better understand the opaque world of platform business models.

I have been pleased to discover the refreshingly innovative partnership model of LID Publishing. I am grateful to Martin Liu, Sara Taheri, Niki Mullin, Charlotte Hutchinson and Miro Iliev and for the joint communication plans we have drawn up with Ellie Duffus.

Finally, I would like to thank the most influential person in my life, my wife Peta. While rarely involved directly in my business activities, she has provided the stable bedrock for all that I have tried to do. I am grateful to her and to my parents for passing on the Christian values I now share, a lens for assessing what is important and durable.

Vouharte, France
July 2016

FOREWORD

A RADICAL REDEFINITION OF THE BATTLE FOR BUSINESS

Disruption Denial is an exceptional book, sweeping into the commercial, managerial and psychological heart of a business world in turmoil. David Guillebaud opens a refreshingly new window on the opportunity – indeed necessity – that so many businesses and their leaders have before them to prosper amid forces of disruption. Conventional wisdom is turned on its head.

The landscape of successful business has changed. Since the industrial revolution began in England more than 250 years ago, we've had a pretty good run. Apart from some serious setbacks associated with war and financial collapse, our economy and the businesses that have increasingly powered it have grown steadily. Technology has evolved and old things have been made obsolete, but generally new developments have been shared, bringing attractive opportunities to all and growing the economic pie, with commensurate benefits for jobs and real incomes.

Over the last few decades, the picture has shifted. Productivity and income growth in the most developed economies have slowed; many tried-and-tested businesses are facing existential threat. New information and communication technologies have transformed consumer behaviour, produced some famous new digital business competitors, but, more than anything, have brought disruption to established businesses struggling for a new generation of profitable growth ideas. The late 1990s technology boom launched the forces of the digital economy we see today, and these have been hollowing out the prospects of many other businesses. Those threatened can't afford to hide in denial; they have to find a new way.

More than a decade ago, when I first had the privilege of working with David Guillebaud, he said something to me that struck a lasting chord: "It's the curse of rampant managerialism," he said, in his understated yet penetrating way. David and I were in the midst of helping an organization's CEO unwind the habits and assumptions of many decades to achieve a desperately needed turnaround in performance. The managerialism reference was to the wading through treacle found in countless organizations, where highly experienced, capable managers were consumed with the stewardship of well-intentioned activity and so-called best practice process, working ever harder but typically achieving diminishing impact and satisfaction as the competitive environment became ever more challenging. In a modest way, David and I made it our mission to try to help leaders break this cycle, and our business advisory endeavours together ensued. I saw first-hand David's insight in action and I am thrilled he has now captured some of it in this lively book.

The author has lived the cycles of rise and fall, success and struggle of the business world across many countries, industry sectors and not-for-profit organizations since the 1960s. His rich variety of business experience, combined with a mind equally attuned to references from the arts, culture, religion and the natural world, enable him to paint a concise, thoughtful and illuminating canvas on the nature of disruption, denial and response.

Readers are shaken from complacency via insights drawn not only from the likely suspects of the new internet-based sharing economy, but also from sources as diverse as missionaries and architects. Alongside thinking inspired by business gurus, this analysis is enriched by insights from fields such as neuroscience and social psychology. Seeded throughout this work is a compelling range of tools and frameworks, which give the reader something to seize and put straight into practice.

Getting under the skin of the world of digital natives, but with a worldly, wise perspective of a much longer tenured business eye, the first part of *Disruption Denial* presents an incisive overview of the disrupted economy. In part 2 on denial and part 3 on survival, the author brings forward a distinctive thesis on the why, so what and what to do. Concepts such as, the "stuckness predicament" and "inbreeding syndrome" are compelling in their capture of typical barriers to change, for which the author goes on to suggest possible remedies.

This is an original and important contribution to rebooting the status quo. It is a book for the vast majority of business leaders who do not have the scarce good fortune, if that's what it is, to ride the wave of new digital economy success stories. It is for those on whom the lion's share of our economy and prosperity depends; those who lead, or aspire to lead, the organizations, large and small, that provide most of our products and services, and employ most of our people. Many of these organizations are at risk of becoming moribund. David Guillebaud offers plausible ways of making them marvellous. This is a call to arms that, while never underplaying the tough realities of making organizations better, is fundamentally optimistic. This optimism is founded on faith in people who have the potential to set aside conventional constraints and follow a refreshed vision.

At the root of the book is the recognition that all organizations are based on people. I have long been puzzled as to why many organizations take great human beings and create constructs, with the good intention of being "professional," "business-like" and "objective," which ironically make it harder to get the best out of those talented individuals. David builds, in particular, on the fascinating research of Frederic Laloux to explore the intriguing field of new evolutionary organizations and ways to make them truly sing.

Disruption Denial: Why Companies are Ignoring the Disruptive threats That are Staring Them in the Face will open eyes and minds. It is a welcome intervention to help organizations, through transformed leadership behaviour, break the constraints of denial and drive the next wave of business value creation and sustainable economic growth. This book will change your business's competitive prospects.

Stephen Warrington

Stephen is an accomplished observer and practitioner of business and management in both advisory and executive roles with, wide-ranging experience. Educated at Harvard Business School, he has been a partner at McKinsey & Company and PwC and led Diamond Management & Technology Consultants in London. He has served as group strategy director for Barclays Group and led an international technology business, chaired an executive search firm, acted as investor and board member for internet start-up businesses and held roles on the boards of academic and not-for-profit organizations.

INTRODUCTION

"Don't they see the existential threat?" someone asked.

"They know there will be a car crash, but they seem mesmerized and cannot turn the wheel!" said another.

"They are in denial!" I replied.

In the autumn of 2015, my wife and I were enjoying lavish hospitality, delicious food and excellent local Bordeaux wines with close friends – three fellow INSEAD alumni and their wives. We were comparing notes on the way business is done these days, as compared to when we began our careers. I found myself explaining that in recent years, seemingly accidentally, I had found a niche in the field of so-called digital disruption. I explained that I have conversations with CEOs and top teams across several industries about the nature, scope, scale and pace of (mainly digital) disruption to established enterprises such as theirs. I asked out loud why it was that so many people I met agreed with what was happening and the nature of the threat, but seemed to be paralyzed, unwilling or unable to do very much about it. As we prepared for bed, Tim said: "David, you know this is an important topic – you should write a book!" He repeated this the next morning and Francois and Henk said the same.

So here we go!

The main focus of this book is the behaviour of top executives in established enterprises as they confront, or ignore, the fundamental forces of disruptive change that will affect their businesses, and particularly the tendency toward denial. While I will be examining the forces of disruption to provide a context for this, I will look closely at denial. If we can understand why it occurs, we can better appreciate how to move forward toward acceptance of reality and responsive action.

Most people are well aware of the digital technology revolution, not least as it affects their own personal lives. Most businesses have some kind of digital transformation programme underway – multichannel, personalization, social, big data, mobility, cloud, data analytics, replatforming the business, you name it. But most are finding fundamental transformation difficult. It seems complicated, costs a lot of money and takes forever. And the internal organization is so resistant, not so much the so-called "digital natives" and practitioners "at the coal face," but the raft of middle managers and functional staff across the organization. Making the case for the investment to the board can also be difficult unless immediate, reassuring benefits are apparent.

Nothing new here, I hear you saying. In fact, throughout my own business and consulting life, I have presided over transformation programmes of all types. Most have disappointed.

When I talk to CEOs and top executive teams about this, we discuss the impact of disruptive innovations, developed further in part 1 of this book. For example, how unlimited storage of big data within the cloud, combined with deep learning algorithmic analysis capability and unimaginable processing power are a game changer for gaining decision-making insight from data. And how the successful business model is no longer about pushing value one way to targeted consumers, but about opening up your platform to consumers, and being part of their and their friends' ecosystem of preferred products, services and experiences.

I introduce them to the work of Professor Clayton Christiansen of Harvard Business School (Christensen, 1997). He showed that even well-managed companies are incapable of reacting to disruption, even when it's staring them in the face. Truly disruptive moves are made by start-ups, which adopt new low-cost business models and use new value networks outside those that incumbent businesses have developed. Over time, they move from their seemingly unthreatening niche into the mainstream of the business of established companies. I say they can do this at a fraction of the cost and by using the best of digital resources, and meet customer needs better than you will ever be able to do. We talk about Amazon's dominance in physical distribution, how companies are outsourcing customer insight to Google, and Apple's move into business sectors. We discuss Kodak, Nokia, RiM, EMI and Blockbuster. It's funny how there is always a reassuring argument why such things would not happen to us, our brands and the investment we have made.

Things get a bit trickier when I suggest that the disruption will be not only in new products and services enabled by new technologies and value networks, but also in *organizational* innovation. Successful disruptors adopt high-performing organizational forms with minimal hierarchy. Employees want to change the world (or at least their industry) and will do what it takes to do so! Many of the service and support functions of established organizations will be delivered more accurately by algorithm-assisted means – and this will mean great swathes of staff becoming redundant. Robots will take over the intelligent brain of your company. "Yes, but" is what I hear.

Most people take it all on the chin. Few disagree with the premise that fundamental change is on the way and that their businesses face an enormous challenge in being able to respond. But few seem to have a clear idea of what to do about the potentially existential threat of fundamental disruption to their businesses, and some do not seem to care, as they may not be in their roles for the long term. They have lots of reasons to rationalize, ignore, wait and see, stick to their knitting, and pull up the drawbridge.

That is why the main theme of this book is denial (part 2). Of course, not all enterprises are in denial; there are striking examples of companies doing radically transformative things. However, many are in denial. What is it about our makeup and how we breed and evaluate our senior people that seems to make denial the default setting when disruptive change is staring us in the face?

This is not meant to be a story of despair. After denial can come acceptance, and then the "patient" can take responsibility and move forward. And there are things that can be done; but they are challenging, since the whole of the established order may seem to be against us. This is the theme of part 3.

PART 1

WHAT ARE THE FORCES OF DISRUPTION AND WHAT DO THEY MEAN?

CHAPTER 1

DIGITAL DISRUPTORS – A NEW BREED OF COMPETITORS

In the introduction to James McQuivey's excellent book, *Digital Disruption: Unleashing the Next Wave of Innovation* (McQuivey, 2013), Forrester Research's senior vice president of idea development, Jeff Bernoff, wrote, "A new breed of competitors has arrived: digital disruptors. These companies and individuals embrace digital tools and platforms to get closer to customers and engage them more deeply. These competitors can come from anywhere and, unopposed, they will steal your customers and disrupt your business." In a nutshell! But I would add the words "perhaps fatally."

Disruption will be direct and indirect. Direct substitution will occur to established value networks – think photography, music downloads and online retailing – but also indirect disruption through innovation in every support function for established businesses. This will affect the production line, in logistics, and through auditing, market research, safety management, customer services and every business process one can think of. Innovators will be, and indeed are, doing things better and cheaper. Disruption is not only happening to vulnerable companies in services or information-rich businesses, but to all industries and sectors. Forrester's McQuivey demonstrates the immediacy of the threat from disruptive innovators to established enterprises and their reach into the bowels of the businesses. Not even highly capital-intensive industries such as mining, aerospace and mass transportation are immune.

New businesses can achieve scale fast. In the past, McQuivey points out, disruptive innovations took years, even decades, to affect markets. Innovation required massive investment and scale to become profitable.

McQuivey wrote, "Disruptive innovation changes all that. But not just in software apps. In fact, the power of digital disruption is that it can disrupt any aspect of a product or service, including processes deep within companies focused on physical things, processes that govern partnerships, data collection, pricing, and the management of labour or capital resources. In fact, digital's power multiplies precisely because it can apply to industries that are not even digital. In this way, digital disruption happens *to and through* digital things, which then accelerate the disruption of physical things."

And digital disruption to traditional business models is irreversible – a bit like a nuclear reaction, once it starts it is almost impossible to contain.

In the science parks of major universities, small businesses are reinventing across the spectrum of life sciences and medical devices. Algorithmic analysis of vast pools of digitized data speeds up diagnostics and experimentation.

Small teams are driving innovation in robotics, machine learning and the "internet of things" within consumer electronics and on production lines, often in collaboration with manufacturing powerhouses. Government labs are becoming open to collaboration with start-ups and small businesses, not just with industrial enterprises. Retailers and financial institutions are coming to grips with the analysis of vast quantities of structured and unstructured data to provide proactive analytics to support customer experiences. In short, the whole innovation landscape is opening up and changing fast.

DISAPPEARANCE OF BARRIERS TO ENTRY

The five forces doctrine of Michael Porter of Harvard University (Porter, 1980) remains a strong influence in business strategy development around the world. The most attractive market segment, we learn as we look at one of these forces, the threat of new entrants, is one where barriers to entry are high and exit barriers are low. In other words, few new competitors can enter, and nonperforming firms can exit easily.

Many of us have immediate experience of friends, colleagues and even family members who have "gone digital" in some way – launched a website, designed an app or launched a digital business. I bet you were surprised how effortless it seemed and how successful simple concepts and business models turned out to be. Of course, we may not be so aware of the failures on the way – they do not talk about them.

Herein lies the reality: historical barriers to entry, such as high capital investment, no longer exist. Even brand equity, customer loyalty and product differentiation can only resist for so long.

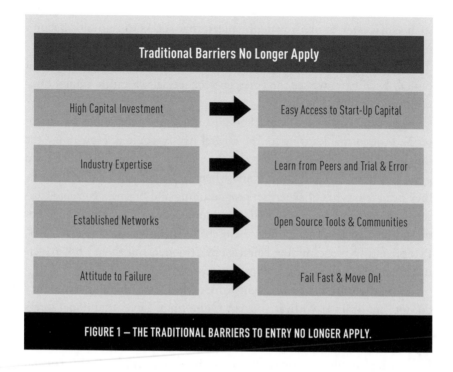

FIGURE 1 – THE TRADITIONAL BARRIERS TO ENTRY NO LONGER APPLY.

Start-up capital. Even in recent history, such as during the so-called dot-com boom, acquiring start-up capital was difficult. I know; my exciting new venture, dreamticket.com, ran out of cash before it could prove itself.

Take software apps, the starting point for many digital entrepreneurs. What is needed?

- A computer and a decent internet connection; most of us already have these. What else?
- A programming language: Apple's SDK (software development kit), a hundred dollars or so to access the Apple store, some reading and some trial and error with the SDK (or the Android equivalent).
- A platform to access interested customers worldwide: the internet, YouTube, Facebook or eBay, which are all pretty much free, ubiquitous and painless.

Compare this with the blood, sweat and tears – let alone capital – needed even ten years ago (*see Figure 1*).

So much for apps, but what about funding real business ideas? They do need start-up capital, but most are funded informally, through friends and family and informal networks. And crowdfunding platforms such as Kickstarter or Crowdcube mean that access to capital is becoming mainstream.

Once an innovation has proved itself, of course it needs development capital. Even here, we see the emergence of specialist venture capital businesses and funding models.

Expertise. For the millennial and post-millennial generations (see chapter 3), little formal learning for the Digital Age is required. How to use the internet and digital tools seems to be the air they breathe. They learn from peers and from trial and error. If and when they want to launch a business, they need two types of expertise: programming and business entrepreneurship. Digital entrepreneurs need some knowledge of programming, but do not have to be programmers themselves. There is a pool of Java, C++, Python and D programming language practitioners out there who are getting trained in a wider range of institutions.

What about business entrepreneurship? Most start-ups fail because they do not "get business," I hear you say. Quite right. Here, traditional forms and sources of learning required to launch a digital enterprise are themselves experiencing disruption. I was struck the other day by the attitude of a high-flying consultant in one of the top firms. Determined to set up a digital business, but without a clear business idea, she is taking a leave of absence to learn how. Not the entrepreneurship courses at INSEAD, Harvard or London Business School for her; she was joining a 15-week Start-Up Tribe programme in London, taught largely by successful digital entrepreneurs. She gets the teaching as well as a community of common interest, and coaching on launching a real business from people who have done it.

Nontraditional support networks. Open-source software, SDKs and a wide range of digital tools have broken down the culture of secrecy in innovation. No longer do innovators need to sweat away on their own in a garret or garage to conceive their creations. They can immediately be members of both online and physical support networks, where they can meet like-minded creative people, discuss and resolve technical issues, share experiences and feel the excitement of a joint endeavour.

Silicon Valley, California, was the first and remains the most striking of the physical communities. One cannot help but be struck by the buzz of the place, as innovators and entrepreneurs interact with venture capitalists, data scientists, programmers, journalists and politicians – you name it. This physical hotbed of creativity is now mirrored in similar groupings around the world: Silicon Roundabout in London, Tel Aviv Start Up City,

Silicon Beach in Melbourne, Silicon Fen in Cambridge, England, Silicon Glen in the central belt of industrial Scotland, Silicon Alley in New York City and others. Start-up hubs exist in most cities these days. (Mainly young) business creators inhabit common space with other budding entrepreneurs, sharing experiences, ideas and concepts around the desktop and the coffee station. Hanging out at locations such as WeWork, TechHub and countless other coworking spaces is the new normal for many.

The online communities are also vibrant. Whether it be through supplier help lines or blogs or communities of common interest or social networks such as LinkedIn or Facebook, someone useful to talk to is not far away. You can use knowledgeable online friends to cut through the noise as a "curator" to direct you to the right person.

The reality is that established enterprises have real difficulty in offering a similarly stimulating creative environment within their workplaces.

Failure is not costly. "Give it a go," I heard recently in a cooperative of social entrepreneurs. A great idea and demo had just been presented to a peer group with some, but not much, of a business plan. And they will indeed give it a go. The concept and reality of open-source software, flexible digital development tools and agile development approaches all contribute to this culture. If it doesn't work, try something else. It is all about learning, experience and building networks, and a confidence that something good will happen. Again, it is a culture that is miles away from what any corporate innovator can hope to create.

DISRUPTORS DO NOT DISCRIMINATE

Disruption does not only affect "old economy" industries. Companies like Nokia, RiM/Blackberry or Blockbuster, seemingly all-conquering a few years ago, were disrupted by new business models and value networks.

In 2001, I had a vivid personal experience of this. I was brought in to advise the European CEO of Razorfish Inc. to help organize the wind-down of operations in Europe. Here was a business that started from nothing in 1994, and had 2,000 employees and a stock price of $57 per share six year later. But it crashed to a value of $1 per share by 2001. From cradle to grave (or at the very least the emergency room), from disruptor to disrupted in seven years!

Razorfish was a glamour business, expanding organically and through an acquisition spree behind the banner of "Everything that can be digital will be," acquiring an enviable reputation for outstanding graphic design work on the internet, innovating in animation and attracting the best talent. What happened? Online graphic design evolved from a highly specialized niche skill to a commodity, driven by the explosion of demand during the dot-com boom. The disruptors were a multitude of small web shops, which could deliver websites with good design and functionality for a fraction of the price – daily rates of $100 as compared with the $1,500-plus fees of the gold-plated service of Razorfish. The company survived, having passed through several owners and now has been re-established as a full-service agency within the Publicis Group. At the time, however, the staff in the Razorfish businesses in the UK, the Netherlands, Germany and Scandinavia seemed shell-shocked, as we were forced to put them into administration or to sell the entities to the management teams. How could it have happened so fast, they asked themselves?

The salutary lessons are there for other recent innovators, such as telco companies like Vodafone. How can mobile service providers reinvent themselves, as they seem to have become commoditized utilities for carriers of voice and data, being disrupted by a range of digital providers of bundled and media services? What is the future for pure-play smartphone makers? Where is the innovation as manufacturers struggle to find added features and consumers just want a machine out of the box without add-ons? Smartphones are levelling off in terms of size, pixel resolution and features, and manufacturers are struggling to differentiate themselves. And there is no obvious "next big thing." Perhaps wearables, smart clothing? They continue to operate in a world and mindset of incremental innovation, with new features and add-ons. This is sustaining innovation rather than disrupting it!

EVERYTHING ABOUT ESTABLISHED ENTERPRISES IS ANATHEMA TO DISRUPTORS

For most entrepreneurs who start and grow disruptive businesses, leaving the corporate world of the established enterprise is a positive choice. They want to create a climate within which they and the colleagues they choose to associate with can thrive and express themselves freely. They don't want all the "stuff" of hierarchical organizations – bureaucracy, time-wasting meetings and paperwork, the competitive culture and the lack of listening to new ideas. Many despise the values of established enterprises: enriching shareholders at all costs, short-term targets, the culture of evaluation and the greed of the idiots at the top. You name it, they do not like it. In fact, in the Silicon Valley world, the MBA is becoming somewhat frowned upon – "Why didn't you just give it a go and learn on the job like the rest of us?"

Charles Sarda and I are both councillors in the local council of our small village in rural France. Charles has developed a small but highly respected web design business called Agence42. When we were discussing digital innovation, Charles put it to me this way: "You have to unlearn everything you were taught in business school and experienced in companies. I and all my fellows rely on the guidance of David Heinemeier Hanson and Jason Fried in their handbook for small businesses, *Rework* (Hansson, 2010)."

A simple but challenging (for old guys like me!) series of aphorisms, *Rework* describes the anticulture of disruptive businesses, and an alternative recipe for success.

Hanson and Fried talk of the development of their successful business, 37signals, now serving three million customers around the world, a company they have kept deliberately small, and for which they get continual criticism from the business establishment: "These critics do not understand how a company can reject growth, meetings, budgets, boards of directors, advertising, salespeople, and the 'real world,' and yet thrive. That's their problem, not ours. They say you need to sell to the Fortune 500. Screw that. We sell to the Fortune 5,000,000."

Or later on: "Embrace the idea of having less mass... Mass is increased by long-term contracts; excess staff; permanent decisions; meetings; thick processes; inventory (physical and mental); hardware, software, and technology lock-ins; long-term road maps; office politics... avoid these things whenever you can. That way you will be able to change direction easily. The more expensive it is to make a change, the less likely you are to make it."

They say you must tell it like it is – plans may be useful, but call them "guesses." After all, this is what they are. A "plan" mindset hamstrings you.

This matters. Because even if you wanted to try innovative start-ups yourself, you are unlikely to be able to attract and retain the creative entrepreneurs you need.

And even if you try to create a climate for creative innovations internally by, for example, establishing "skunk works" below the water line, so to speak, out of sight of the main enterprise, this will not work for long. As soon as it is successful, the organization will want to interfere and want to embrace it. The "dead hand" of the mother will smother the baby.

ESTABLISHED ENTERPRISES CANNOT DO DISRUPTIVE INNOVATION

Face it: disruptive innovation in all its forms will happen, especially outside your enterprise.

There's nothing new about disruption. The Austrian economist Joseph Schumpeter (Schumpeter, 1942) wrote about "gales of creative destruction" in the first half of 20th Century as a way of describing the markets' way of making progress by disrupting established paradigms. Disruptive forces, mainly technological, have driven successive waves of innovation. These waves have accelerated over the past 200 years, and with them the rate at which enterprises that have refused to adapt have been destroyed.

Many of the leaders of the successful digital enterprises which so dominate the business landscape today – Apple, Google, Amazon and Microsoft – were strongly impacted by a seminal work written by Clayton Christiansen, then professor of business administration at Harvard Business School back in 1997. "Don't worry; established enterprises are asleep at the switch. They are unable to respond." This was how they interpreted what Christiansen's research seemed to be saying – a reassuring message (for them). While there has been some criticism of the methodology employed by Christiansen in his works, few are challenging the underlying doctrine and theory.

In *The Innovator's Dilemma: When New Technologies Cause Great Firms to Fail* (Christensen, 1997), Christiansen looked at late 20th century disruptive innovations: disk drives and excavating equipment, for example. His conclusions challenged the established orthodoxy that business failures are due to bad managers not keeping up with technology. He showed that well-managed firms are usually aware of the new technological innovations. But the way they do business does not allow them to pursue disruptive innovations when they arise. These are not profitable enough at first. The way firms plan and allocate resources stops them from pursuing such innovations because it would take scarce resources away from sustaining innovation in products and services to existing customers, which are needed to compete against current rivals. And any such investment would not be justifiable against established investment criteria.

On the other hand, start-ups have different business models and value networks. They can use the new technology to deliver value to customers in different ways, usually at significantly lower cost. Incumbents leave the start-ups freedom to operate since they are incapable of responding.

In other words, even if you see disruptive innovation about to happen, your established organizational form will be unable to react. Unless you can change, you will suffer a "death of a thousand cuts" – inevitable, painful and lingering. Melodramatic? Perhaps.

CASE HISTORY – THE EUROPEAN LOW-COST CARRIER (LCC) AIRLINES

In the mid-1990s, my colleagues and I were working closely with a number of major European airlines, including British Airways and Lufthansa, on means to adopt emerging internet technologies to transform their distribution and in-airport productivity – electronic distribution, and reinventing the in-airport check-in and departure experience. We had grandstand seats as we watched the Christiansen doctrine being played out in the European aviation industry.

The Context

Initiated in 1992, the European Union finalized the deregulation of "Open Skies" in Europe in April 1997: any technically qualified airline in the European Union (plus Norway and Iceland) could run services to and from any other EU country. This was no surprise; everyone knew it was coming, and everyone knew what was likely to happen. After all, similar deregulation had been introduced in the US in 1978 and the lessons were there to be learned. This saw the rise of low-cost carriers (LCCs), such as Southwest Airlines, with a different value network – no frills, point-to-point flights (as opposed to hub-and-spoke) often from secondary airports, direct online booking, and fast turnaround in airports leading to massively improved utilization of standardized aircraft, all resulting in huge reductions in the price of tickets. EasyJet already existed and was offering a Southwest-like service (on which its founder, Stelios Haji-Ioannou, had modelled it) with apparent success.

As if it were yesterday, I can recall a senior executive saying: "This is a different industry. Our customers are looking for a premium service when they fly on regular services to major destinations. They do not fly to secondary airports. We mustn't get distracted and must stick to our knitting. After all, there have been many catastrophic failures in the US and few successes. Southwest is a special case."

But the impact of the LCCs did not take long to create casualties. In 2002, I was directly involved in the fallout of the bankruptcy of Sabena. The pride of Belgium, with a wide network and routes to several African destinations, Sabena was unable to survive through difficult times, not least because of the impact of Virgin Express operating out of Brussels, and Ryanair operating out of a new base in Charleroi (marketed as Brussels South by Ryanair). Between them, these LCCs were stealing the lunch of Sabena on short-haul routes and compromising feeder traffic to the profitable African routes.

The Belgian establishment rallied round and put together a group of 40 investors, and my colleagues and I were commissioned to evaluate possibilities. We were able to make a business case for a lower-cost new airline to be recreated on the foundation of DAT, the regional airline daughter company, which was not in administration. The new airline could marry the best of the low-cost model with the best of the Sabena heritage (but not the costs). Brussels Airlines became a success out of the ashes of Sabena, in fact merging with Virgin Express in 2004 to create a strong carrier based out of Brussels. In 2008, Lufthansa acquired a major stake in Brussels Airlines, which is now a full member of the Star alliance of airlines.

A Technological Innovation Propels a New Business Model

A fundamental but simple digital innovation blindsided them – not just the freedoms for LCCs to operate to, from and within any European country, but the arrival of a reliable, innovative, hosted airline reservation and revenue management platform focused on direct distribution to low-cost operators. Supplied by companies such as Open Skies, and later Navitaire and others, these platforms allowed customers to book online and for the airline to price the ticket on the basis of a yield-managed algorithm – i.e., based upon predictions of demand for specific flights at different assessments of capacity utilization.

There was nothing new about yield-managed pricing; this had been introduced by the major airlines decades earlier. However, they had very low levels of direct sales, relying upon travel agencies (both business and leisure) to effect bookings across the platforms of large Global Distribution System (GDS) enterprises. Travel agents took hefty commissions and GDSs demanded expensive transaction fees. The yield management algorithms for pricing different "buckets" of allocated seats (10 or more categories in some cases) were focused upon maximizing revenue at the front of the plane (first class and business class) and incentivizing travellers from remote locations to connect at company-dominated airport hubs. In fact, the connecting flight to and from the secondary location to the hub was often pretty much free, so long as the long haul revenue between hubs was optimized; this was a very different philosophy from that of the LCCs.

Trapped within the framework of bilateral agreements between designated "national flag carriers," combined with the need to offer destination-to-destination tickets between countries and airports, the industry created its owned Global Distribution Systems (GDS) organizations, and set up complex arrangements within the industry body, IATA, for distribution of ticket revenues to each airline used by travellers on connecting flights. These GDS companies became highly profitable in their own right. American Airlines created Sabre, British Airways created Galileo, and Lufthansa and other airlines created Amadeus. When American Airlines was in financial trouble and needed to dispose of assets, the legendary Bob Crandall, chairman and CEO of American Airlines, was quoted as saying, "If I had to choose between owning an airline and owning a GDS, I would own the GDS!"

However, the booking and ticketing service of GDS companies became clunky and inefficient, and the technology was not designed to meet the simpler direct-sales model of LCCs. GDSs were forced to reinvent themselves under different ownerships and became providers of a wide range of IT and hosting services to airlines. But that is another story. In any event, in the late 1990s, Southwest and others were more than ready for the new platforms.

While some network airlines dabbled in the LCC model at that time – in the case of British Airways, with Go! and KLM with Buzz – the conflicts in focus and measurement became obvious and the national carriers largely ignored the LCCs, standing on the sidelines as they grew exponentially.

In the meantime, easyJet, founded in 1995, went from strength to strength. More spectacularly, under the leadership of Michael O'Leary, who had studied the model of Southwest, Ryanair transformed itself from a small Irish airline flying selected routes into the most profitable airline in Europe.

Growing Threats to the Core Business of Legacy Airlines
Christiansen's work also tells us that while start-ups initially create new business models within different value networks and are largely ignored by incumbents, it is not long before they are able to invade the older value networks, and with a significantly better-performing business model. And this is what is happening here.

The real and present danger to network airlines is not so much their profitability within an activity they have largely ignored, but that the LCCs are now encroaching into the mainstream activities of network airlines – the front of the plane and network feed. "Eating into the tasty but soft underbelly of what makes traditional airlines profitable," an industry insider told me.

Up until a few years ago, the network carriers were resigned to the reality that the majority of nonbusiness travel under three hours flight time (leisure and visiting-friends-and-family) would be the preserve of the LCCs, and they could concentrate on the needs of more loyal business travellers on these routes and serve them for connecting flights to long-haul destinations. Today, most LCCs are offering an acceptable business class product and decent frequencies to major business destinations. They siphon off a significant share of business travellers from the network carriers. EasyJet is rolling out a simple loyalty programme for frequent travellers, offering perks that are as attractive, if not more so, than the cumbersome benefits offered by the loyalty programmes of airline alliances.

A journey with Vueling offers you an airport and flight experience among the best of short-haul in Europe. A start-up LCC a few years ago, Vueling became part of Iberia when it merged with the Iberia-owned LCC Clickair and became a sister company to British Airways in the IAG group upon the acquisition of Iberia. Was this a fortunate accident, or shrewd strategic design? In theory, Vueling is well placed because it can retain much of its low-cost heritage and gain added advantages from the purchasing power of the BA group. But will its cost structure and culture be subsumed by the parent?

Perhaps more importantly, the LCCs are moving into the territory of schedule coordination to enable the feed to network carriers for their profitable long-haul flights. Carolyn McCall, CEO of easy-Jet, feted the company's 20th anniversary in November 2015 with the announcement that the airline was going a step further by holding discussions with network airlines about providing transfer connections for their passengers – more formal schedule coordination, through ticketing, and potentially even code-share arrangements.

What is the role, if any, for short-haul legacy brands in this scenario? Total disruption for legacy national flag carrier brands beckons.

The same story is playing out in industry after industry. And disruption is not only digitally led; sometimes it can be a different business model altogether. For example, grocery retail in the UK is an example of disruption to the established players in which digital technology did not play a role.

EXAMPLE – UK GROCERY RETAIL

The big four UK players – Tesco, Sainsbury's, Asda-Walmart and Morrisons – were seemingly oblivious to the threat of the deep discounters from the continent, Aldi and Lidl, when the latter first entered the UK market in the 1990s.

These continental players entered with a disruptive business model: a scaled down, in-house range together with quality products at low prices. The stores had low levels of technology and a basic shopping environment for customers, often characterized by aisles of pallets piled high with products. Providing offers, which were not deemed comparable to market leaders in terms of range, service and convenience, they were largely ignored as they began to nibble at market share.

Now, more than two decades later, they are a very real threat and have established themselves as a genuine competitive presence among the well-known grocery leaders, with a combined market share of 10% (Tesco has 28%, Asda 17%, Sainsbury's 16% and Morrisons 11%). Aldi has 500 UK stores and aims to double this over the next six to seven years, while Lidl has more than 600 and is opening around 30 to 40 new stores each year.

They have disrupted the high street with a new business model, forcing the big players to reevaluate themselves.

CONCLUSIONS ABOUT DIGITAL DISRUPTORS

This new breed of innovators, mainly digital start-ups that may grow rapidly into substantial and valuable enterprises, will be a new kind of competition. Not competition that you can combat with the weapons you are familiar with, but competition to the very model that underpins your business, and the value networks and relationships you have built.

These competitors deploy digital tools and platforms to get closer to customers and engage them more deeply. They can come from anywhere and, unopposed, they will steal your customer and disrupt your business, perhaps fatally. They will not only disrupt your direct business model, but also how you operate your business, affecting the functions and services with which you operate.

The management system and processes, which sustain your enterprise and which you have built up so assiduously over the years, do not help; in fact, they are a hindrance. They force you to focus on sustaining incremental innovation, and discourage you from disruptive innovation. Consequently, almost inevitably, you will underestimate, even ignore, disruptive digital business models, even if they are obvious.

But all is not lost, so long as you recognize these realities, develop antennae to detect disruptive innovations, both existing and potential, and prepare yourself for response. But more of that later!

CHAPTER 2

DISRUPTION OF BIG DATA, ALGORITHMS AND ROBOTS

We have all heard about Big Data. A Google search tells us that these are "extremely large data sets, which can be analysed computationally to reveal patterns, trends and associations, especially relating to human behaviour and patterns."

We know about the exponential growth of data availability of all types and that the storage possibilities in the cloud mean that phenomenal amounts of data can be processed and made available in real time. We know that clever things can be done by powerful computers to manipulate and interpret the data. Most companies have spent small fortunes on creating data warehouses of mainly customer data, and many have developed data analytics capabilities in order to gain business insight from their data.

It is not my intention here to go into technical depth on the topic; there is a wealth of research and writing on the subject of Big Data out there – see the references at the back of this book for a useful set of links to further resources provided by IBM (IBM, 2016). But I do contend that the scope, scale and pace of the technological revolution derived from Big Data and the algorithms applied to interpret it have been severely underestimated. I will explore those aspects, which will tend to disrupt traditionally structured enterprises and highlight the challenges they face in embracing the opportunities. First, some context.

THE EARLY DAYS

Many of us were introduced to the power of Big Data more than 15 years ago by Apple's iTunes. When you purchased and downloaded music, a Genius bar popped up that made recommendations on other music to buy, based upon what other people like you had bought. Amazon did the same when you bought a book. We became fully at ease with having suggestions made on what to buy. What was going on here? Online retailers were able to track what customers bought, their browsing behaviour on the site, what else they looked at, how they navigated through the site, and what notice if any they took of reviews, promotions and page layouts. They were able to compare all this knowledge about a customer with that of other customers, in order to predict what they were also likely to be interested in. In short, they applied algorithms to the data collected by one's usage of the site to predict what books individuals would want to purchase next. As the volume and sources of data grew, both on their sites and from outside, their predictions became more accurate. They were personalizing their store for us. And we were not unhappy to have a personalized service.

It reminds me of an analogy from the offline world. When a good suit salesperson in a traditional high-street store is selling men's suits, he has hundreds on the racks in all sizes, designs and styles. When a customer enters the store, the experienced salesperson sees the size and shape of the customer, his age, the kind of fabric and style of apparel he is wearing, his colour sense and so on. He is immediately able to pull out the few suit options likely to appeal to that individual customer from the hundreds of theoretical alternatives available. This is much what the online retailer is doing: scanning data, applying knowledge and triggering response. But imagine if the salesperson had at his fingertips or in his eyesight the information that told him about the wider likes and preferences of the customer, and not only of this customer but of millions just like him.

WHAT HAS CHANGED? THE FOUR VS

From those early beginnings, we are now in a magnified data world (*see Figure 2*).

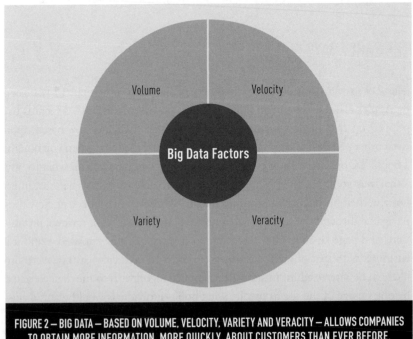

FIGURE 2 – BIG DATA – BASED ON VOLUME, VELOCITY, VARIETY AND VERACITY – ALLOWS COMPANIES TO OBTAIN MORE INFORMATION, MORE QUICKLY, ABOUT CUSTOMERS THAN EVER BEFORE.

VOLUME

The sheer scale of the growth in data availability is difficult to get one's mind around. Attempting to estimate this is futile and outside the scope of any normal person's comprehension. To get some kind of handle on it, I like the example quoted in the *Harvard Business Review* in October 2012, stating that Wal-Mart collects more than 2.5 petabytes of data every hour from its customer transactions alone (McAfee, 2012). A petabyte? It is one quadrillion (one thousand million million) bytes, or the equivalent of about 20 million filing cabinets worth of text. Every hour! Just Wal-Mart! Just its customer data! Four years ago!

Furthermore, digitization of data of all sorts is growing exponentially. Everyone is doing it – libraries, school curricula, medical notes, research papers, you name it. Sensors are being installed everywhere, producing real-time flow of additional data: weather updates, traffic vibrations, body function diagnostics, road vibration, tidal movements and so on. Drones are collecting data not previously easily accessible. Nanoscience opens up the potential to insert microscopic sensors and processing technologies within the human body itself!

A key question is how all this volume will be stored and managed, and by whom. And importantly, how security will be assured and data (particularly personal consumer data) be protected.

VELOCITY

While Big Data volumes are growing exponentially, and the types of data proliferating, the speed at which they are being created has been outpacing many organizations' capacity to handle and analyse them. And the stakes can be high for interpreting data in near real time, and vital for deriving value. If companies can get there, real-time insightful analysis of collected data can yield astonishing results. For example, on the trading room floor of a financial institution, having a stock quote or a prediction of a trend one-thousandth of a second faster than a competitor can make all the difference.

Fortunately, the Big Data beast can be tamed. Storage in the cloud, massive increases in computing power and ever-improving analytical tools now increase the speed of the potential availability of insightful information exponentially. Thanks to new approaches for processing, storing and analysing massive volumes of multi-structured data – such as Hadoop and MPP analytic databases – enterprises of all types are uncovering new and valuable insights from Big Data every day.

VARIETY

Big Data can be internal and structured, such as e-mail of customer trans-actions or images posted to social media, and also be semi-structured and unstructured. There can also be relevant data out there on the so-called "dark web," where companies should not be present! Such relevant data may be both internal and external to the enterprise. Indeed, for business, massive amounts of relevant data exist outside the enterprise – on mobile phones, social networks such as Facebook or Twitter, on GPS, on comput-ers and tablets, in electronic communications and on sensors in electron-ic machinery, including household appliances. And we can acquire these data, either raw or treated, from specialized organizations like Google, and include them in our own analytics. In fact, it is scary how specialist organ-izations are able to collect data about us from these sources and apply their behavioural analytics algorithms to produce accurate predictions. One company I have worked with claimed to increase the conversion rate for a visit to a travel website from 5% to more than 25% by applying its tool. But more of that later.

VERACITY

By definition, Big Data are big! They can also be messy! Getting a clear signal within the noise is critical – cleaning out the bad data from the good becomes vital. Here, computer analytics is invaluable. By rapidly detecting patterns in the data, the machine ignores, or deletes, the data that do not conform to the pattern. However clean data sets become a reality only if the best analytical treatment is applied.

THE "DEMOCRATIZATION" OF DATA

Yes, companies have never had as much data as they do now. Many have developed specialist business analytics teams that seek to ensure that useful insights emerge from the noise and are brought to light in the decision-mak-ing processes of the firm. But the Big Data beast is becoming uncaged. It is becoming democratized – available for use, and misuse, throughout the organization. Powerful, easy to use, and inexpensive programs are becoming widely available, allowing workers in the organization to comb through large data sets and identify meaningful patterns themselves.

Democratization of data opens up new challenges to organizations. They do not want to see people making flawed interpretations and bad decisions based on decentralized data. After all, people can find virtually anything out there to support an argument. The issue of control rears its head – whoever controls the data controls the decision! This fear can lead analytics teams to clamp down on who can access the data and how much individuals can see. As a result, more business questions end up funnelling through the analytics team for answers. Then analytics teams have the challenge of scaling sufficiently to handle the increasing volume of data-related questions coming from internal users. Analysis paralysis becomes a reality!

THE POWER OF ALGORITHMS AND ARTIFICIAL INTELLIGENCE

Algorithms and the notion of artificial intelligence have been around a long time. However, it is the ready availability of large digitized data sets, combined with efficient storage in the cloud and massive increases in computing power, which now bring them to the fore.

I first became aware of the power and potential of algorithms back in the late 1990s when I invested in a start-up called Xaim. Jeff Brandt and his team came out of a statistical analysis group in the US aerospace industry and their goal was to apply statistical analysis techniques to the diagnosis and treatment prognosis of cancer – in the first instance, prostate cancer. Applying neural networks methods to laboriously compiled nondigitized medical records, supplied by the American Cancer Society and Cancer Research UK, the Xaim algorithm was able not only to detect patterns in patient files linked to outcomes, but also to identify determinate factors in the data for the onset of prostate cancer. Many of these factors were new, even apparently crazy, compared with the medical lore of the time – including ethnicity, location of residence, diet and sleep patterns, as I recall. The algorithm was also able to learn and improve the accuracy of prediction as the data set grew and was used. By comparing treatments to outcomes in thousands of actual cases, the diagnosis accuracy from the widely used prostate-specific antigen (PSA) blood test and the doctor's finger was computed to be only 25% or so at that time. By using the Xaim desktop application and inputting the additional factors the data analysis had discovered into a desktop application, the doctor could secure diagnosis accuracy of 60% or so. Unfortunately, Xaim went the way of many start-ups at that time, running out of cash as the medical profession showed resistance to adopting new ways. Xaim was before its time. In the Big Data era, applying its algorithm would be a piece of cake. However, the resistance of the medical profession may not have changed!

With Big Data, executives have not only more digitized data to work with, but also the processing power to handle large numbers of records with many attributes. Developments in technology make this possible – for example, Big Data analytics in the cloud, the emergence of new enterprise data operating system standards such as Hadoop, data "lakes," and alternatives to traditional relational databases better adapted to predictive analytical applications. And there is now "deep learning."

THE DEEP LEARNING REVOLUTION

Deep learning is seen as the next big thing within the Big Data field. We are now seeing concepts of artificial intelligence (a label somewhat discredited by many) taking shape within deep learning and becoming applied to massive data warehouses within enterprises, now being relabelled as Big Data "lakes."

Deep learning takes the application of statistical techniques such as neural networks to the next stage. These neural networks model the behaviours observed in the human nervous system. They enable computers to recognize items of interest within a vast, unstructured binary data lake and to deduce relationships without needing human intervention, programming instructions, nor use of predefined models. In simple terms, the machine tells us what is important and can prompt us to make decisions, based on the data that are shown to be important. What the machine tells us is important may be surprising, counterintuitive or even seemingly irrational. And the quality of the output improves over time as the machine learns from usage. This is what Xaim was doing for prostate cancer, but this can now be done at great speed and with larger and better digitized data sets.

Using these techniques is not new. Apart from Xaim and applications to other medical records, these techniques are already used in facial and speech recognition, language processing, audio recognition and bioinformatics, for example. What is new is the emerging use of these deep learning techniques within fields affecting established commercial enterprises.

REBIRTH OF VIRTUAL REALITY

In the early 1990s, my colleagues and I were commissioned to innovate the experience in visitor attractions and museums. We worked with innovative architects in the early stages of "virtual reality." We participated in the design and installation of simulators in theme parks and interactive displays for the curation of museums. In those days, the immersive experience was limited and the technology pretty basic. That being said, I remember an afternoon in a warehouse in a Brussels suburb in a mocked-up cinema set. We sat in motion-induced seats, put on wired gloves and helmets, and tested various permutations of technologies aimed at inducing a multisensory experience. It was all a bit artisanal, but it felt quite exciting nevertheless.

Fast forward to a recent visit to the Gaudi Exhibition Center in Barcelona, in early 2016. Here you can sit down with a helmet that has a Samsung smartphone strapped to the front and look down on a 360-degree reenactment of Antoni Gaudi's workshop during the early stages of the construction of his visionary Sagrada Familia basilica. Okay, the picture quality was milky and the visual quality a bit jerky, but here was a truly captivating 360 degree immersive experience, an example of the potential of a new consumer market.

Developers have not paid as much attention over recent years to virtual reality as they have to the development in other exciting fields enabled by the convergence of the mobile telephone and consumer electronics – such as applications for the iPad and Android. After all, the scale impact of apps made the breakeven of developments easy to attain, so you could see the fruits of your labours early. But with the launch of the Oculus Rift headset, retailing in the US at $599, many observers are predicting lift-off. Indeed, Goldman Sachs predicts that the VR market will be worth $80 billion by 2025.

Cheaper virtual reality sets like the one I used in the Gaudi Exhibition Center, linked to smartphone, such as Samsung's Gear VR and Google's Cardboard, have come on the market offering what is still a rather basic VR experience. But the Rift headsets allow high-quality, super-immersive virtual reality viewing in a small package – a remarkable innovation for those in a space that has been stagnating for so long.

Understandably, much attention has been paid to the social dangers and the lack of any regulation of this "new" industry – particularly for pornography. But, there will be more serious applications in the fields of teaching, training of the workforce, medical sciences, research and development, films and video games, not to mention in gaming and a multitude of online applications and experiences. As one VR geek put it to me recently, "You ain't seen nothing yet! There is no limit to how VR will impact our world – in manufacturing, logistics, research and development, education and medical sciences. Wait and see!" So you will need to keep an eye on VR!

THE ARRIVAL OF THE EIGHT-HUNDRED-POUND GORILLAS

Now eight-hundred-pound gorillas (Apple, Google, Facebook, IBM and Microsoft) are putting their massive paws into the Big Data arena!

Many of us use the Siri function on our iPads or iPhones and do not think twice about the neural networks, which sustain this service. Google is undoubtedly the leading force in Big Data, having search and predictive behavioural analytics capabilities and access to networks of partners that we can only imagine. In 2014, Google made a significant move by paying $400 million (small beer for them) to acquire Deep Mind Technologies, a London company specializing in artificial intelligence (Regalado, 2014). Deep Mind's stated goal is to combine "the best techniques from machine learning and systems neuroscience to build powerful general-purpose learning algorithms." This could be game changing. In Google Now, Google already uses predictive analytics to combine location data with calendar entries, emails and past search queries to predict what the consumer will do next. The app then displays pertinent data on the tablet without the user being asked.

Most of us are aware of how Facebook can package up profiles of whom you are based upon your usage and sell this to advertisers. But Facebook has nowhere near as much data as Google. Google announced the relaunch of Google Plus in November 2015 with additional communities (where people can share common interests) and collections features (enabling collation of things you love). Google can predict a huge amount about you, and what you like, by tracking your usage across their different platforms – Gmail, YouTube, Google Maps and Chrome. Then if you volunteer additional interests, they have an astonishingly accurate picture of whom you are – an invaluable commodity to advertisers that can target their communication with pinpoint precision. Even if you don't volunteer additional information about yourself, it is scary how accurate their profiling can be! Before long you will be watching on your tablet and TV a totally personalized channel of content and advertising that fits with "you."

Deep Mind adds an additional intelligent capability to sustain Google's wider ubiquitous computing vision. This will include a power grid, smart homes, high-performance personal computing devices, robots, electric cars and other transportation, all linked together by "learning machines" customized to each organization, business or individual user.

DISPLACEMENT OF JOBS BY MACHINE

"Man as machine" is being displaced by "machine as man." Use of robots on the production line is now so commonplace that we hardly notice. Bank of America predicts that 45% of all manufacturing tasks will be automated within the next ten years, up from 10% today (Zega, 2015). The International Federation of Robotics says the number of robots in factories around the world rose by 225,000 in 2014 (Prodhan, 2015).

In November 2015, Andy Haldane, the chief economist of the Bank of England, was speaking at the Trades Union Congress in London (Haldane, 2015). His was a wake-up call to the representatives of organized labour in the UK. He explained that over the next 20 years, a new generation of increasingly creative, smart machines could put rafts of traditional clerical, administrative and production jobs at risk. Up to half of the 33.7 million jobs in the UK will be at risk. In the US, up to 80 million jobs are "at risk of automation."

The BBC website offers a user-friendly tool that brings to life the potential of displacement of different jobs by machine automation over the next 20 years (Nassos Stylianou, 2015). Applying algorithms to data collected by researchers at Oxford University and Deloitte, the site shows that about 35% of current jobs in the UK are at high risk. You can type in your job title, and any other job title, and see the computation of how much the job is at risk of displacement by automation.

Within the algorithms lies the "learning" that more advanced industrial robots are gaining the ever-greater capability to make more coordinated finger and hand movements, and to manipulate and assemble objects. They will be able to perform a wider range of increasingly complex manual tasks. And analytical tools can replace an array of intelligent tasks and functions at work.

By studying the BBC's output, it is clear that emotional intelligence (EQ) will be more important than IQ as a risk factor in the potential of replacement by machine. So, where empathy is important (carers, therapists, nurses, social workers), the risk of displacement by automation is low. Creative jobs requiring reaction to circumstances in real time, such as artists, designers or engineers, will also be resistant to automation. Furthermore, roles requiring a high degree of social intelligence and negotiating skills, like general managerial positions, are considerably less at risk from machines, according to the study – a somewhat reassuring personal message for the senior executive cohort we are concerned with! In contrast, while certain sales jobs like telemarketers and bank clerks may involve interactive tasks, they do not necessarily need a high degree of social intelligence, leaving them exposed to automation.

Deep learning algorithms will indeed be capable of replacing a number of office and administrative support roles, particularly in legal and financial services. For example, the legal profession is already experiencing the efficiencies derived from machines carrying out tasks undertaken by legal professionals by scanning thousands of documents to assist in pretrial research.

CONCLUSIONS ON THE DISRUPTION TO ESTABLISHED ENTERPRISES

Is this a 20-year or a 10-year vision? How imminent is this all? Who knows? Enterprises must be clear, however, where and how they fit and add value in that scenario. And they need to anticipate and deal as best they can with the disruptions that will result to their existing business model. Here are some of the disruptions.

1. New Decision-Making Paradigm

In the recent past, when data were not digitized, scarce, expensive and clunky to obtain, we liked to rely on the best-placed persons in the organization to make the decisions – based on analysis of the data, yes, but also based upon the intuition of the deciders derived from their experience in the domain. In practice, in most organizations the decision has been taken by what the data community is calling the "HiPPO" – the highest-paid person's opinion!

Even in organizations that have made a significant financial commitment to Big Data and analytics, it is rare to find HiPPOs who are genuinely data-driven. Senior line managers rarely come from a data analytical background. Few are prepared to let the data override their intuitive opinion. This leads to a waste of a precious source of competitive advantage and to continuous poor decision-making.

2. "Outsourcing" of Customer Knowledge

Much of the data and insight, which an established enterprise needs to compete in the data-rich world, will reside outside the company, within the purview of the 800-pound gorillas. Research from the premier global market intelligence firm, International Data Corporation, shows that by 2020 80% or so of the digital data universe will be generated from users (consumers or workers creating, capturing or replicating personal information), and 80%+ of the content will be managed by the enterprise platform managers such as Google and Facebook. And only a small proportion (approximately 13%) will be generated within the enterprise for its own use (IDC, 2014).

There is also a multitude of new intermediaries servicing the interface between their platforms and business partners. One example of such a player is Clicksco. A multi-million dollar "adtech" company based in Dubai's Media City, Clicksco is a "leader in the mining and manipulation of big data in the retail, finance and travel sectors," as their website says. "We turn clicks into customers," they claim. Clicksco collects and analyses massive lakes of offline and online data, and they will no doubt be one of Google's biggest customers – but also a major customer of telephone companies, as they sell mobile phone usage data, and of social networks such as Facebook and Whatsapp. Their website explains that they are able "to precisely understand who these people are and what they are interested in buying. We use this knowledge to drive people to sites that can answer their needs, turning web traffic into sales." So, more customers, higher conversion rates online. And all this without, I suspect, yet being able to deploy the latest generation of deep learning algorithmic tools.

The necessary reaction to this goes beyond hiring a smarter digital marketing agency. It requires a mindset shift – accept it, you have a miniscule amount of usable knowledge about your customers compared with the Googles and the Clickscos of this world. It was not so long ago that companies talked of "owning the customer." If anyone can be said to own the customer today, it is the 800-pound gorillas and their families. Your role is now to embrace the reality that real customer insight lies elsewhere and to open yourself up to the massive lakes of data so you can fit in to the "ecosystem" of needs and relationships that the individual customer or business partner require.

3. Redundancy of Swathes of Management and Central Staff Jobs

Top executives are on the case as far as the employment consequences of production robotics are concerned. This is what competitiveness and productivity are about and installing automation is very much in their comfort zone. And use of robotic machinery to replace manual labour in nontraditional industries is also very much on the increase – e.g., remote picking of fruit. And this is okay too. Discussions with unionized labour about downsizing through redundancies and retraining are routine, even though sometimes fractious.

Many traditional industries have been slow to respond as technology advances and disruptors disrupt – why do Air France and other legacy airlines need staffing levels of pilots and cabin staff so much higher than low-cost carriers, and with much higher salaries and perks? How can this be sustainable? And in industries affected by the sharing economy – Uber, Airbnb – traditional taxi businesses and accommodation concepts are so disrupted that old models and job levels cannot be sustainable. It is only for so long that unionized labour and regulation can hold back the tide.

From my observation, most senior executives are much less accepting of, let alone prepared for, the creeping and soon-to-accelerate replacement of humans working in support functions inside enterprises. After all, these are "people like us!" This is true not just for jobs that we have become accustomed to seeing displaced – clerks, secretaries, telephone operators, bookkeepers and typists – but also intelligent jobs, such as in business analysis, IT, finance, auditing, quality control, market research, logistics, communications, even supervisory jobs and middle management. In the 90% probability of replacement by automation band on the BBC website tool, we find telephone salesperson, financial accounts manager, bookkeeper/payroll manager/wages clerk, and financial accounting technician – no surprise here, perhaps. But when you get down to the 50% automation risk band (perhaps a sensible level for active consequential planning), you hit upon middle-management jobs – manager or director of key operational support functions – such as storage, warehousing, purchasing, transport and distribution, and IT engineers, credit controllers, and health and safety officers.

The future enterprise will have fewer but more highly skilled employees. There will be two forces at work – outright replacement of man by machine and reskilling of other employees in surviving jobs.

Some active planning and retraining initiatives are surely needed, given the reach into the flesh of the established organization that all this implies. Perhaps this might be a resource base for retraining in disruptive innovation spawned by the enterprise itself? (*See chapter 12.*)

CHAPTER 3
DISRUPTIVE CONSUMERS

Last summer, we had a whole tribe of children, grandchildren and their friends – more than 20 of them – sitting at a long table on the terrace of our home in France. Different generations, with some members speaking different languages, were all enthused by being together, the balmy evening, the great food and wine, and reflections on the different activities of the day. My wife and I love these occasions – it seems so rare these days to connect with the tribe at a deep level. We got to talk about meaningful things: education, the police, politics, terrorism, life/work balance, and God. It was fascinating. Particularly, how different age groups look at these things through different lenses. It was like they were looking into a room through different windows – exactly the same furniture, carpets, doors, knick-knacks, light and shade, but they saw the room differently, they processed what they saw differently, and they reached different appreciations of what they saw. They were displaying generational bias.

And these new generations of consumers are also disrupting the traditional world of established enterprises.

Let us have a look at the type of consumers with whom established enterprises will need to engage (*see Figure 3*).

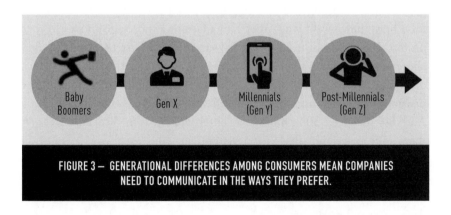

FIGURE 3 – GENERATIONAL DIFFERENCES AMONG CONSUMERS MEAN COMPANIES NEED TO COMMUNICATE IN THE WAYS THEY PREFER.

With apologies for the generalizations and simplifications, this is one way of segmenting customers, but you could argue that this too has been disrupted! Lifestyle and behavioural segmentations are now critically important to our understanding of consumer behaviour and clustering on age is a crude mechanic that runs the risk of hiding many of the idiosyncrasies – I know people well into their 70s who display traits of millennial consumers, and similarly people in their teens who could be considered luddites! I know everyone is different, but having said that, people tend to take on some characteristics of their generational tribe. I believe the generalizations help to understand the trends that established enterprises ignore at their peril.

THE BABY BOOMERS

Most traditional enterprises in the Western developed world were established by, are managed by, and existed to service the needs of Baby Boomers. These are those people born in the immediate years after World War II, when there was a significant spike in births thanks to soldiers returning from war. But the phrase is now used to cover all people born from 1945 through the early 1960s – in other words, consumers who are between 50 and 70 years old today. By some calculations, more than 75% of C-suite executives are from this generation – across all industries in North America and Europe, with little variation between countries. After all, it does take time to climb the greasy pole!

This was a blessed generation. It was the UK Prime Minister Harold Macmillan who put it succinctly in the 1950s: "You have never had it so good!" After revolting and swinging in the sixties, most parked their ideals for a brave new world when they had a family, a mortgage and a career to protect. Most did not need to fight a war. In most Western countries, they had cradle-to-grave welfare and healthcare. Many got rich without much deserving effort by the spike in real estate values. They have or will have pensions that generations before and after could and will only dream about. And they may have 30 or more years of retirement, as medical advances give them a life expectancy that they never anticipated.

Of course, many were not blessed in this way, and deprivation and sadly poverty continue to abound across our societies. However, the Baby Boomers had the consumption muscle – they were the original targets for product developers and marketers.

Baby Boomers tended to have faith in scientific rationalism. Human ingenuity, combined with advances in technology, would solve all the world's challenges. In October 1963, the UK's Prime Minister, Harold Wilson, delivered a famous speech at the Labour Party conference. He captured the mood of the Baby Boomers and their modernist worldview when he called for Britain to be forged of the "white heat of a technological and scientific revolution."

THEN CAME GENERATION X

Generation X consumers were born between the early 1960s and the early 1980s. These thirty-somethings to early-fifty-somethings grew up absorbing the realities and values of their parents, but were forced to adapt to a less rosy world than that of their Baby Boomer parents. Sometimes referred to as the "latchkey generation," they got on the "property ladder" on their own account, negotiated mortgages, and invested in property and stock markets. They were more independent and self-sufficient than the later millennial generation – they took charge of their careers with little involvement from their parents.

Not particularly entrepreneurial or risk-taking, Generation X consumers became strong managers within traditional organizations. Indeed, they populate the middle management of a wide range of enterprises and within public service. A Gen Xer is a "safe pair of hands."

Socially, the avatar for this generation is the six well-groomed adults in the sitcom *Friends*, who in many ways embody this generation's behaviours and values. Too young to have fought in a war, old enough to have benefited from free education and universal welfare, they tend toward ennui and cynicism – i.e., a state of mind characterized by distrust of other people's motives. "What's their angle?" they tend to think. Gen Xers' cynicism was reinforced by their lifestyle – too much time spent in coffee shops, obsession with diet and fitness, and regretful ennui that they have tried to put the world to rights and have failed. They suffer from anxiety of all types – their body, their sexuality, their friends, their place in the world, their financial situation, you name it.

Generation X consumers tend to be postmodernists in their worldview – distrustful that science has all the answers, more disposed to spirituality (as distinct from organized religion) and highly individualistic. They tend to reject the way we do politics, the way we do business, the way we do religion, the way we look after the planet, the way we do schools – in fact, the way we do most things. They are natural members of the Occupy movement and proliferate in the new political movements emerging to the left of politics in Europe, even if they are not necessarily left-wingers politically.

A powerful industry of consumer research grew up to segment this generation into target markets and to understand their needs. They gravitate to marketing messages that understand their particular needs. I am "me"!

THE RISE OF THE MILLENNIAL CUSTOMER (GENERATION Y)

Also labelled Generation Y, millennials were born between 1980 and 2000. In 2015, millennials became the largest demographic group in history. Many commentators predict that they will represent 75% of the global workforce within ten years. Aged between 15 and 35, their purchasing power will shortly overtake that of the Baby Boomers.

Millennials are the first generation to grow up poorer than their parents. They have become accustomed to a less stable and predictable world than that of their parents. They have been impacted heavily by geopolitical upheaval and from social and economic unrest – this has consequences for their career opportunities and earning potential, and has fired up their social consciences.

I am indebted to Micah Solomon's 2015 article in *Forbes* magazine (Solomon, 2015) where he identifies five characteristics of millennials as customers, which are worth summarizing here, not least because they illustrate the gap in understanding, and therefore in potential denial, of the executive classes (mainly Baby Boomers).

Millennials expect technology to simply work – so make sure that it works. They despise any interface and system that is old-fashioned or clunky. All they know are digital devices that bundle communication, entertainment, shopping, mapping and education all in one. Smartphone use has been the norm. According to Pew Research, four out of five sleep with or next to their smartphones (PewResearchCenter, 2010) and they use them for texting and everything else more than any other generation.

Millennials are a social generation – and they socialize while consuming (and deciding to consume) your products and services. They congregate in groups both online and offline – they shop, dine and travel in these groups. Online they share habits on Facebook and other social networks, and they are eager for connections. According to marketer Jeff Fromm, Solomon says: "They don't make a major decision until they have discussed it with a few people they trust." Surprisingly, they get along with their parents, in fact their "group advisory" behaviour is welcomed by their parents, who take their advice on what to buy!

They collaborate and cooperate – with each other, and where possible, with brands. Millennials have a positive, community-oriented "we can fix it together" mindset. If they sense that they matter and are listened to, they want to collaborate with brands they trust – in fact, they identify with these brands and don't really distinguish between the brand and themselves. So companies that figure out how to engage with this cooperative relationship will win out.

They are looking for adventure – and whatever comes their way. They want to travel the world, they want shopping to be a memorable experience regardless of whether they buy anything, and they expect dining to be a memorable experience with their friends almost irrespective of the food. Normal is boring.

They are passionate about values – including the values of companies they do business with. This is perhaps the attribute that distinguishes them the most and should be of greatest interest to companies interacting with them. They feel strongly about civic values. They are concerned with political and ethical issues. They care about authenticity. Unlike Generation Xers, they are optimists, not cynics, but they distrust vacuous marketing – they are searching for honesty and truth.

GENERATION Z (POST-MILLENNIALS)

Yes, of course, there must be a Generation Z! Born just before the start of the millennium, they are in their teens. Too young to remember 9/11, they are growing up in a world of political and financial turmoil, of terrorism and insecurity. Sparks & Honey, a US advertising agency, describes this generation as the "first tribe of true digital natives" or "screenagers." They are potentially smarter, safer and more mature than the Generation Y, but they want to change the world. One of their idols is is Malala Yousafzai, the Pakistani educational campaigner, who survived being shot by the Taliban and who became the youngest-ever Nobel Peace Prize winner.

They are keen to volunteer and to help. According to Sparks & Honey's research, sixty percent of them want to have an impact on the world, as compared with 39% of millennials (Peterson, 2014).

CONCLUSION: THESE NEW CONSUMER GENERATIONS CHANGE THE WAY YOU MUST LOOK AT YOUR BUSINESS

Millennials and post-millennials represent the future customers of your enterprise. Their world is the tablet-accessed, personalized ecosystem of products, services and experiences that they consume with their friends. They trust brands that their friends trust, but they can be promiscuous, migrating to new brands and experiences, which their ecosystem gravitates to. They are prepared to open themselves up to companies they trust. They will also discard companies they consider to be out of date and offering clunky, low-performing technology.

Unlike Baby Boomers, who are obsessed with the dangers of cyberspace and the internet, they are more sanguine about cybersecurity – this is the reality of the online world they inhabit. They are also more comfortable using data as their currency to interact with businesses.

Put simply, they live in a "platformed ecosystem" world. So this is the world that established enterprises must offer them. But the replatformed back end must also be complemented with a high-performing front end, where all the elements of attractive user interface linked to social networks and community building are present.

Building the right products, services and experiences in response to the desires of these consumers and their friends, you need to recognize that human beings (salespeople, customer service people) may not help – in fact, they get in the way and complicate their experience without adding any value. The new generations of consumers are comfortable with technology that eliminates human intermediation. This will be disruptive to your sales and distribution organization.

You must open up your company, its knowledge and systems, to these new consumers and their friends. You will be rewarded, because this will be two-way traffic. As you help them to contribute to their ecosystem of preferred relationships, brands and experiences, they will exchange their ecosystem with you. This will be a mutually beneficial exchange of value creation.

The journeys consumers take and the experiences they seek have also moved on. The funnel analogy to sales is no longer appropriate. After the impulse to buy is triggered, customers no longer narrow the decision-set of brands in a funnel-like way as they progress through the purchase journey. All touch points now represent an opportunity for companies to enter the decision-making process for these consumers. The brands they evaluate expand rather than contract as they continually revaluate what they want in light of cues they receive from social media.

The post-purchase experience is now hugely influential in determining customer loyalty. Under the influence of social media, a good or bad experience will have deep repercussions on other consumers considering and evaluating purchasing the product.

The loyalty of these new consumers cannot be "bought" through loyalty schemes in the same way it was with as previous generations. Your company's social influence, or "clout," becomes more important to these consumers than the benefits you might offer through loyalty and retention schemes.

CHAPTER 4

DISRUPTION TO BUSINESS PLATFORMS

THE TRADITIONAL MODEL FOR DOING BUSINESS

We have all grown accustomed to business models, which are composed of an operating model and revenue model (*see Figure 4*). This forms the basis on which nearly all companies operate and compete.

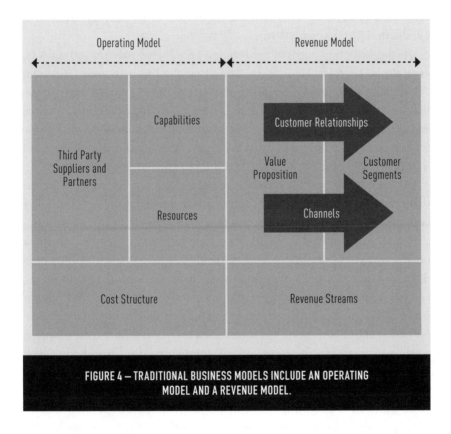

FIGURE 4 – TRADITIONAL BUSINESS MODELS INCLUDE AN OPERATING MODEL AND A REVENUE MODEL.

Over the years, companies will have spent fortunes building up proprietary IT infrastructure, processes, systems and organizations to make this business model work efficiently. Product and service offerings designed to meet the needs of targeted customer groups were developed on these IT platforms, and the whole organization was supported by systems and processes crafted to deliver value efficiently, to provide management with the information it needed to guide the ship, and to meet internal and external reporting and compliance obligations.

IT departments became critically important parts of the enterprise, since they needed to continually improve the business model machine as the business activities evolved, and to keep it oiled and responsive to the needs of the business. IT departments were very often seen in the early days as a "keep the lights on function" rather than strategically important. Then businesses began to recognize that IT belongs at the top table. In fact, some have gone so far as to redefine themselves as technology firms (e.g., Goldman Sachs, L'Oreal, Ford).

As the scope and needs of the business grew, new hardware and software capabilities improved, and costs of meeting the business needs escalated, IT seemed to take on a life of its own, often seemingly unresponsive to the needs of business units and unable to deliver improvements on spec, on time and on budget. A massive IT services industry grew up to provide costly services to support internal IT departments, effectively throwing people and money at projects to improve and speed up the developments needed.

As the internet and the Digital Age became more prevalent, it was clear that established enterprises were at a disadvantage from the new pure-play entrants, which developed new business platforms using the latest infrastructure, tools and technologies. Everyone knew that they had to throw off the costly and inefficient burden of their clunky "legacy." Companies often invested in a layer of "middleware" to sit on top of legacy systems, equipped with application programming interfaces (APIs) so that systems could better interact with each other and be accessible to digital users. People talked about "shrinking the legacy" as a means to render their obsolete, costly and inefficient business models competitive in a world for which they were not designed. All too often these replatforming efforts resulted in disappointment and failure as the complexity that had built up over the years rendered a successful outcome unlikely. Moreover, the skills needed to support these legacy systems depleted as technologies moved on and the capabilities to support them retired: the "human glue" that bound them together began to lose its potency.

In short, they struggled to have a capability fit for operating their business, fit for purpose in the Digital Age, and fit to deal with the cumulative "archaeology" of legacy systems and the resulting technical debt that had built up.

THE PLATFORM REVOLUTION

Then, almost unseen, along came the platform revolution. It snuck up on most of us and caught many unawares. In 2000, I was chairman of a travel software company with a growing reputation in delivering software solutions for the internet and digital media. Our business model was based upon earning royalties from licensing proprietary software. We developed applications for our clients on this basis. Suddenly, open-source software became the rage. External developers could develop software applications on someone else's infrastructure!

Apple led the way with the iPhone, with its cool features and functions. But their success, and later that of Google's Android-enabled smartphones, was not about features and functions. After all, Nokia and Blackberry had great products too, and look where they are now. No, the success of Apple and Android-enabled smartphones came from the open platform they created for others to use – the app store on which external developers could create value – and with the idea of the "extended enterprise," the platform ecosystem was born. Gone were the days of the enterprise having to "own" its supply chain. Now organizations could leverage the network effect by developing platforms for a plethora of other businesses to leverage. Developers could quickly master the software development kit provided by Apple or Android to build their applications and gain access to the store at an easily affordable price. In fact, you did not even have to be a died-in-the-wool computer programmer to do this.

Transformative technologies accelerated the move to platforms. The cloud provided the borderless infrastructure for production to a global audience, mobile allowed access to this infrastructure at will, and social media connected people online. Digital native consumers became avid adopters. Big Data and algorithms opened up the infinite possibilities for product creation, innovation, personalization, sharing and significantly automated decision-making.

A digital platform behaves in the same way as a platform in the construction or offshore oil industry - it provides a common, stable base on which others can do their work. It opens you up to other businesses, so that they can easily connect with you and enables them to build products and services on it and you can co-create value with them. And it opens you up to customers both known and unknown who want to buy what meets their needs (and who can help you adapt what you offer to their needs). You become part of an open ecosystem.

Platform thinking became the modus operandi of innovators in other sectors. For example, Amazon, Alibaba and eBay led the way in online retailing. Nike now offers the Nike+ platform to companies to build new products. Amazon has its marketplace to connect buyers and sellers without having to assume liability for the stock, and eBay operates in a similar fashion, connecting demand and supply across a vast range of categories.

In contrast to the traditional model, composed of additive layers – infrastructure, data, applications, processes and organization (out from which pop product or service offerings that are pushed out to targeted consumer groups), a platform business opens up all of this. Interfaces to the data lurking within the layers allow external people – customers, suppliers, partners – to customize what they want and at the same time join with you in an ecosystem of co-creation of products, services, experiences and value (*see Figure 5*).

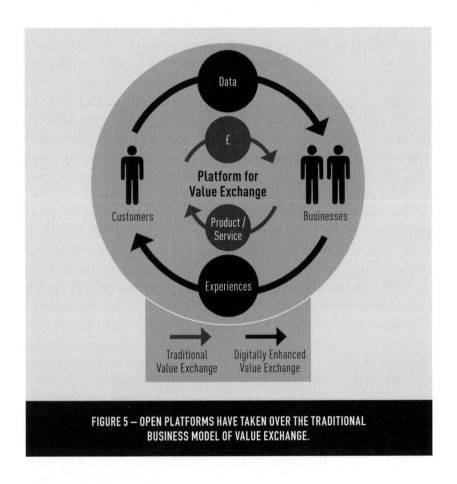

FIGURE 5 – OPEN PLATFORMS HAVE TAKEN OVER THE TRADITIONAL BUSINESS MODEL OF VALUE EXCHANGE.

As a producer of goods or services, you would ideally want a platform where you and other likeminded and complementary producers of goods and services can interact with consumers and other partners directly. Others are then playing on your platform, without intermediaries such as Amazon involved. This results in much less value-erosion and your platform business itself retains the transaction value, rather than a third party.

THE EMERGENCE OF DIFFERENT TYPES OF PLATFORMS

In understanding the purpose and utility of a platform, I am grateful to David Mullins of Elixirr for pointing me to the wisdom of Lao Tzu. This great philosopher was describing in his own way what a platform does way back in the 6th century BCE when he recorded his thoughts in *Tao Te Ching*, the important book that underpins the belief system of Taoism. Truly, there is nothing new under the sun! Here, in chapter 11 of this magnificent work, is how he captured the essence of what we are calling a "platform" and how it renders things useful!

> "Thirty spokes share the wheel's hub;
> It is the centre hole that makes it useful.
> Shape clay into a vessel;
> It is the space within that makes it useful.
> Cut doors and windows for a room;
> It is the holes which make it useful.
> Therefore profit comes from what is there;
> Usefulness from what is not there." (Addiss, 1993)

Wow! The usefulness of your platform is what it enables – the interactions between you, consumers and others in the ecosystem. Profit will come from your platform ("what is there") because of the usefulness of interactions that take place on it ("what is not there").

Different types of platforms have emerged over the years (*see Figure 6*).

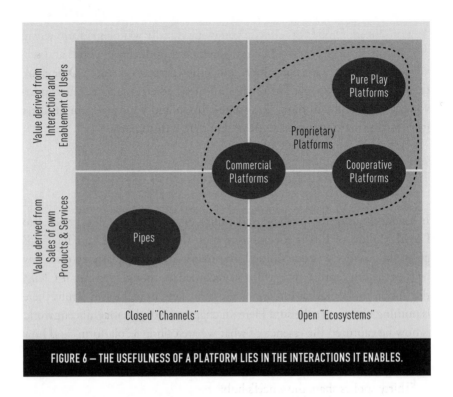

FIGURE 6 – THE USEFULNESS OF A PLATFORM LIES IN THE INTERACTIONS IT ENABLES.

Pure-play platforms. These include Apple and Google, social networks such as Facebook, Twitter and Whatsapp, and music, video or music-sharing platforms, for example. They also include sharing economy platforms such as Airbnb. These are enabling an infrastructure on which interactions of all kinds can take place between providers and consumers – communication, sharing and exchange. Take YouTube, for example. Here is a high- tech platform – its usefulness, and consequential profit, come from the value people achieve in sharing and viewing videos in an ordered and intuitive way. To paraphrase Lau Tzu, YouTube is the "vessel" that provides the "space" for users to derive something useful. The profit to the platform owner comes from the usefulness the users of the platform derive – translated by different revenue models such as advertising, data marketing, subscription or whatever.

Commercial platforms. These include Amazon, eBay, Booking, Expedia and the multitude of online stores specializing in different commodities. They share many of the attractive features of pure-play platforms and present beguiling features to customers.

Owners of these platforms are principals – they own or have a direct financial interest in the products and services presented on the platform. They are an online replacement for the physical world. They use the muscle of scale to secure low prices from suppliers. They become a "must be listed" channel for your products or services, in just the same way as a multiple retailer, a department store or a dominant specialty store in the high street. They are into land-grab and exploitation of oligopoly power. Once established, they aim to shut out other competitors.

But you do not have to be an 800-pound gorilla to have an effective commercial platform. Take the case of the online retailer very.co.uk. It recently became the first online retailer in the world to start serving fully personalized web pages to customers – it expects to be offering over 3.5 million versions by the end of 2016.

Cooperative platforms. There are a few, but not many, of these out there – Loconomics, Enspiral Network, Lazooz, On The Market and Swarm are a few examples. They cooperate with other providers and share value with their customers. Unlike the Ubers, which take on and seek to displace the physical world – taxi operators and municipalities – cooperative platforms are owned by their users. Their aim is to create a value-adding marketplace for suppliers and users – real platforms as per Lao Tzu, similar to Facebook in the commercial arena.

There is evidence of growth in cooperative platforms as suppliers of products and services come together to reach their customers directly, and thus loosen their dependency on powerful digital intermediaries. One example of a cooperative platform created with this objective is the Global Hotel Alliance (GHA), an alliance of luxury hotel and resort brands. This is a platform owned by its suppliers, where discerning customers can discover, book and compare notes and recommendations with fellow visitors. They can also get exclusive benefits when they visit other hotels and resorts. Collectively, the hotel owners have a tool that gives them marketing reach, which they would have difficulty achieving individually.

Some real estate agents in the UK have banded together to create a cooperative called Agents Mutual to react against the dominance of property sales portals such as Rightmove and Zoopla. The new portal On The Market is a late-response initiative to claw back what traditional agents perceive as their natural advice-led business.

The sad truth is that most suppliers of products and services have "missed the boat" in the creation of their own cooperative platforms providing benefits to themselves and their customers directly. They have been unable to collaborate – either through misplaced ideas of competition, fragmentation of the industry, or the absence of a lead sponsor to launch and finance the initiative, which may be perceived as highly speculative by smaller players. They have allowed specialist intermediaries to build the commercial platforms instead. Take the case of independent hotels in tourist destinations.

Booking.com has built a fabulous business, meeting the needs of that part of the hospitality industry iceberg that lies below the waterline, the myriad independent hotels from small, family-run bed-and-breakfast facilities to executive apartments and five-star hotels and resorts. Unlike the major groups, these individual businesses do not have the marketing muscle to go to market in the online world on their own. So Booking.com has met a real need – providing a platform for them to do so. Nearly 850,000 properties in more than 220 countries are now listed on Booking.com's site, and nearly one million transactions are concluded every day!

If you are a small chain or independent, you are virtually obliged to be listed on the Booking.com site – such is the market power it has built. There is no doubt that the website offers the consumer a terrific experience – an informative and user-friendly booking site, guaranteeing the best available price. Why go anywhere else?

But at what price to the hotelier? They are obliged to pay commissions of at least 35% and have high dependency from this and other Online Travel Agent (OTA) intermediaries, such as Expedia. You could argue that they are even worse off than they were in the pre-internet age. The opportunity to create a cooperative industry platform for suppliers of in-destination accommodations, activities and experiences has been there for a long time. And who knows, it may yet come to fruition in the form of a partnership between the destinations and the private sector operators who want to get their product to market without the high cost of using value-eroding intermediaries such as Booking or Expedia.

Proprietary platforms. These are mainly bright and shiny front ends to traditional businesses and are what most established brands call their platforms. They may offer many appealing features, including loyalty schemes and opportunities to interact with customers, but they have little of the truly scalable, interactive features of a true platform. They become part of a multichannel or omnichannel strategy.

A NEW MINDSET – THE ECOSYSTEM

The effect of these new platform business models could be devastating on adjacent firms and industries. The "winner takes all" prospect was emerging from new platform businesses like Amazon and Alibaba as they leveraged the network effect. While traditional firms grew their businesses incrementally through classic continuous improvement initiatives, new digital native innovators could use their platforms to extend the reach of their value proposition way beyond what the traditional firms could do, and at a marginal cost approaching zero. At the same time, their value propositions became progressively more compelling, unfettered by legacy systems and culture. It's as if a new predator had arrived at the Galapagos!

Few senior executives have yet wrapped their minds around the fundamental shift in mindset that the ecosystem concept implies.

Yes, companies have to be relevant by having the right products and data available and keep a step ahead of competitors. But the end game is gaining the right to be recommended by customers through social media and being part of their ecosystem of trusted providers and consumers who are free to interact with each other in a trusted framework. This implies a revolutionary shift in mindset and behaviours, which traditional enterprises are ill equipped to deal with.

In his brilliant book, *Platform Scale: How an Emerging Business Model Helps Start-Ups Build Large Empires with Minimum Investment* (Choudary, 2015), Sangeet Paul Choudary describes the revolution underway:

"We are in the midst of a transformative shift in business design as business models move from *pipes* to *platforms*. Firms build products, or craft services, push them out, and sell them to customers. Value is produced upstream and consumed downstream, creating a linear flow of value, much like water flowing through a pipe… Early digital models also followed the pipe design. The first media companies on the internet worked like pipes. Amazon's e-commerce store started as a pipe… even today, many businesses continue to see the internet as a pipe, one of many delivery channels.

"However, three forces today – increasing connectedness, decentralized production and the rise of artificial intelligence – are driving a whole new design for business. The emerging design of business is that of a platform. Some of the fastest-scaling businesses of the last decade – Google, Facebook, Apple, Uber and Airbnb – leverage the platform business model. These businesses create a plug-and-play infrastructure that enables producers and consumers of value to connect and interact with each other in a manner that was not possible in the past. Platforms allow participants to co-create and exchange value with each other. Developers can extend platform functionality using its APIs and contribute back to the very infrastructure of the business. Platform users who act as producers can create value on the platform for other users to consume.

"This changes the very design of the business model. While pipes created and pushed value out to consumers, platforms allow external producers and consumers to exchange value with each other."

Choudary goes on to describe the imperative for businesses to scale the platform: "Business scale… powered by the ability to leverage and orchestrate a global connected system of producers and consumers toward efficient value creation and exchange. The management of the platform scale involves the design and optimization of value exchange between producers and consumers."

Wow. Not exactly what most C-suite executives were brought up to understand!

"STOP SPEAKING LATIN"

In an earlier turning point of history – the Enlightenment – the disruption came not only from an explosion of new ideas, but also from how they were communicated and distributed through the printed word. Renaissance man was expected to speak and write in Latin, which was the lingua franca for all intellectual intercourse, be it astronomy, politics, theology, medicine or whatever. When in 1637 Rene Descartes (Renatus Cartesius, as he was then known) wrote his seminal philosophical statement, "Cogito ergo sum" (I think, therefore I am), he actually wrote in French – *Je pense donc je suis*. I guess he woke up one morning and said, "Why am I writing this in Latin to a small elite of intellectuals, when this is a message for the whole of mankind? So I will write it in French!" This was a revolution that helped usher in the Age of Reason and accelerate its adoption throughout Europe.

Many corporations, boards and top executive teams continue to speak and think in Latin. They think about a business model of pipes – pushing product to targeted consumer groups – multichannel, omnichannel, personalization. But the new *lingua franca* for business in the Digital Age is platforms.

I love the way Choudary summarizes the shift. This is his platform manifesto:

1. The ecosystem is the new warehouse
2. The ecosystem is also the new supply chain
3. The network effect is the new driver for scale
4. Data is the new dollar
5. Community management is the new human resources management
6. Liquidity management is the new inventory control
7. Curation and reputation are the new quality control
8. User journeys are the new sales funnels
9. Distribution is the new destination
10. Behaviour design is the new loyalty programme
11. Data science is the new business process optimization
12. Social feedback is the new sales commission
13. Algorithms are the new decision-makers
14. Real-time customization is the new market research
15. Plug-and-play is the new business development
16. Invisible hand is the new iron fist.

Terrific, but scary! Think about how the platform business model makes many existing functions, not to mention swathes of workers, potentially redundant!

CONCLUSIONS

Can someone be in denial about something they do not know they do not know? A moot point, but I observe from many a widespread denial among top executives about the need to know about the new platform paradigm, and a lack of determination to understand and react.

Established enterprises are going to need to be active participants on all platforms – pure play and commercial – marrying the features with an opening up of their legacy "pipes" model for the platformed ecosystem reality of the disruptive world.

Your new business model will need to marry the best of the old with the innovations of the new. When we talk about "platform," we are not talking just about technology, but all the layers of the future business model: strategy, leadership, technology, people/talent and organization/process.

Building the right business model, at least with important platform features, will be both a challenge and a fundamental requirement for established enterprises. The forces of inertia and gravity are overwhelmingly strong, given where most enterprises start. You cannot fight them. If you try to, failure is the most likely outcome.

This begs the question: "What can you do to beat the odds?" We explore this in chapter 10.

CHAPTER 5

DISRUPTION TO ORGANIZATIONAL ORTHODOXY

Very few top executives I talk to challenge the assertion that the way we generally organize the workplace has become cumbersome, inefficient and wasteful. Indeed, they leap to give examples. I personally have presided either as a principal or as an advisor over transformational programmes across many industries. They have all underperformed or disappointed. Why? I suggest that this is because the model of the "organization as a machine" is no longer in sync with the times.

The way an organization behaves is indeed rather like operating a machine – a professional management cadre in the centre decides, and pulls levers whereby cogs in the organizational machine turn and employees execute. Despite attempts to soften its edges, command and control from the centre within hierarchical pyramids still dominate the general conception of how to organize for work. This may have worked once, but it seems to work much less now.

In an increasingly complex world, ever-increasing layers of systems, processes and controls – while necessary in theory – only serve to "increase the viscosity index" of the oil in the organizational machine, as one CEO put it to me. It requires so much more energy to make the machine turn effectively, it seems. With the growth in education, aspiration and awareness, modern generations of employees are not interested in being components in someone else's machine. They want and need to feel more involved.

In contrast, when I and my colleagues meet with managers of innovative start-ups, we are struck that they are innovating not only in product, service or means of deploying technology, but also, as importantly, in organizational form. They are developing structures in which creativity and productivity can naturally thrive.

If this is so obvious, why aren't corporations adopting different organizational forms more attuned to the modern age? Quite.

A HISTORICAL PERSPECTIVE

Alfred Sloan would, no doubt, have been gratified how his memoir, *My Years with General Motors*, written in the 1950s but published in 1964 (Sloan, 1964), has influenced how organizations, great and small, organize for work throughout the developed world. Accelerated by the demands of economic reconstruction after the end of World War II, the Sloan vision of the professional manager and the carefully engineered corporate structure within which he worked were adopted wholesale for the international enterprises set up to transfer the industrial power and wealth of the United States into Europe and the Far East after the war. Upon Sloan's foundation, scientists co-opted into the military to assist with military operations added techniques of mathematical modelling, statistics and decision analysis to create the "management science" that so dominates the way we view the skills and functions needed to make an organization function efficiently.

As the public stock company took over from other widely applied organizational forms, such as private companies and cooperatives, and the demand for capital to fuel growth grew insatiably, shareholder capitalism became entrenched as the foundation for efficient wealth creation in the developed world. "Management science" became overlaid with the frameworks and structures for decision-making in this shareholder capitalistic world. The concept of "shareholder value maximization" as the framework to achieve and assess performance became king.

The organization as machine adapted to the needs of enterprises at different stages of development – structured by business function, by geographical division, or units by type of business – and matrix structures (hybrids of functional and divisional structures) evolved. However, in all these variants, the hierarchical pyramid structure still underpinned the way resources were allocated and decisions were made.

The organizational model of command and control from the centre by a cadre of highly educated scientific rationalists was in tune with the prevalent modernist worldview of the mid-20th Century. Post-industrial society maintained its faith in science and the emergent disciplines of engineering as the means for human progress. The language of engineering still permeates organizations today. We talk of human beings as *resources*, plans as *blueprints*, about *efficiency* and *effectiveness*, *inputs* and *outputs*.

A whole industry of business administration education developed, first in the US and then around the world, teaching the tools of the trade of the professional manager and the techniques required to oversee a complex organizational machine. An MBA from a prestigious institution such as, for example, Harvard, Stanford, Wharton, London Business Schools, INSEAD or IESE became the passport for a glittering career in management.

No one would surely deny the positive impact this all had on economic development in the decades after the Second World War. Given the dearth of expertise outside America in operating large, complex and increasingly transnational enterprises, applying a formulaic engineering-type approach to supervision of such enterprises, and growing a cadre of executives with the expertise to apply them, made obvious sense and produced positive benefits.

In parallel, banks and other professional financial institutions came to dominate the provision of capital for development and growth and in turn influenced the ownership of organizations. It became apparent that the pathway to growth was to become a public company with an orthodox, scientific, rationalistic organizational form. In fact, no other way of managing a business seemed to exist. Even mutual societies and cooperatives seemed to operate like this. Other sources of capital from foundations, benefactors, philanthropists, or friends and family could not sustain a growing business and banks' attitudes to risk limited the potential of growth through bank borrowing. Once it had proved itself as a successful business, an enterprise had an overwhelming incentive to "go public" in order to gain access to the funding of the capital markets (as well as to enrich its founders).

Once quoted on a public exchange, the business became subject to the rules and constraints of public companies. In many cases, these companies succeeded through investment-led growth and acquisition, fuelled by funds raised on equity markets and (often leveraged) debt. Other sources of capital unlinked to capital markets were limited. It was not until the rapid growth of private equity in its various guises that alternative forms of big capital outside public markets became available. Even while private, they maintained their orthodox organizational form while their new owners found means to restructure operations and the balance sheet to secure a profitable exit. Better human performance within better organizational forms was rarely a priority for these new temporary owners.

"DEATH BY POWERPOINT"

This phrase has become a kind of shorthand for the creeping malaise within organizations of managerial "stuff" – interminable meetings supported by dull, crammed slide presentations. It was the father of advertising, David Ogilvy, who famously quipped, "Most people use PowerPoint like a drunk uses a lamppost – for support rather than for illumination." By extension, it is a metaphor for the progressive decline in effectiveness of the orthodox organizational form, which has served the world so well in the post-war years. Divisional or functional silos became entrenched. Little meaningful communication happened naturally across structures. So central staff functions were created, and internal or external consultants helped prepare plans to be presented in meetings across silos, and so on.

As explained in more detail in the denial section of this book, executives found they had little freedom to chart a long-term course for their businesses. The structures, rules and incentives of a public company within a shareholder capitalistic ownership world forced them to focus on short-term results, on incrementalism, and on their existing business model and value networks. In short, they were trapped within the system, and the orthodox organizational model worked against fundamental and disruptive change. The model seemed to have reached its "sell-by date" – but there seemed to be no real alternative.

The "Law of Unintended Consequences" kicked in, in my view, as early as the 1970s. One example was the detachment of senior executives from the realities of work at the "coal face." We saw the emergence of a stratum of elite "professional managers," both executives and their advisers, living in the rarefied air of the executive suite of corporations, detached from the practitioners at the sharp end of their industry. These managers could segue smoothly across sectors without industry experience being considered important. In fact, quite the opposite, it appeared – *not* having an industry background could be an advantage. "You will have a clear mind and not be confused by industry prejudices," we were told. I was contacted by an executive search firm in the early 1980s in the search for a CEO for a division of a well-known industrial conglomerate. The fact that I had absolutely no knowledge or insight – let alone experience in that complex industry – was an advantage, apparently. Madness!

It was not just in the Anglo-Saxon world that elites of professional managers came to dominate the corridors of power in politics, public administration and business. In the country where I make my home, France, graduates of the Ecole Nationale d'Administration (ENA), dubbed colloquially *énarques*, dominate positions throughout public service. Coming from the most elitist and prestigious school in France, drawing the best of the best from the other *grandes écoles*, the 100 ENA graduates each year are anointed with near-guaranteed positions at the highest levels of the French state. Not surprising, you might say, that this high-powered elite inbreeds common attitudes, remaining detached from those doing common toil within their ministries. In the business world, graduates from the Ecole Polytechnique, dubbed "X," have a similar position. Gaining entry to the

Ecole Polytechnique or another of the *grandes écoles* is a passport to success within public and private enterprises – there is no point in aspiring to senior positions if one does not come from one of these schools.

In his seminal 2007 book, *Unmanaging: Opening up the Organization to its Own Unspoken Knowledge* (Taptiklis, 2007), Theodore Taptiklis gives an insight into what it meant to be a young consultant in McKinsey & Co.'s London office in the 1980s. A member of a kind of Praetorian Guard of the management elite, he and the partners of this blue chip consulting firm glided through the corridors of power, proposing rigorously analysed solutions and strategic plans to executive teams and boards across all industries. The firm became the gold standard for strategic planning, with recommendations often applied wholesale with little if any engagement, let alone understanding, of the employees. Progressively conscious of the detachment from reality of many of these proposals, let alone the inefficiency of ignoring the knowledge and talent lurking unseen within the organizations and the consequential waste, Taptiklis goes on to describe his own journey. He examines the research and writings of savants from many disciplines and professions that so convinced him that leaders need a completely different approach. He suggested how to develop skills to encourage productive encounters within the workplace, and the use of storytelling and listening and learning from stories as means to tap in to the rich, but underused, expertise within the firm.

Perhaps the most significant challenge to the "organization as machine" metaphor was that the workplace behaviours fell totally out of sync with the new generations of consumer described in chapter 3 of this book. Through increasing complexity, the clean engineering concept foreseen by Sloan and applied by Baby Boomers had morphed into a complex of processes, systems and controls, and organizational "stuff" that qualified as "managerialism" by many. A post-modernist worldview began to take hold within later generations, which distrusted the notion that scientific rationalism had all the answers. Employees wanted to be recognized and to express their humanity at work. Many employees found themselves "managing around the system" so as to be able to express themselves to colleagues, customers and suppliers in a way that mattered to them – so the centre was losing touch, let alone control, of the executors of their plans.

The "system" began to recognize this. John Hunt, Plowden professor of organizational behaviour at the London Business School, argued back in 1989 that the biggest mistake a business can make is to treat management as a science, and to treat employees as cogs in a machine. "We have relied far too much on structure, and not enough on gut feel… The scientific rationalist approach has produced a very bureaucratic and regulated society, but what makes people interesting is not just the regulation but the irrational, the emotional and creative side… The belief was that managers could produce a rational scientific system, whereas in fact we know that it is about emotion, about love and hate" (Daily Telegraph, 2015).

REINVENTING ORGANIZATIONS

A whole industry of organizational development and human resources departments, and external consulting firms, has grown up striving to improve communication, collaboration and humanity at work. Everyone gets frustrated – nothing seems sustainable when back at work. It all seems a bit of a charade, like shadow boxing. Nothing can fundamentally change, it appears.

It seems that the personnel practices of a bygone age could be more in tune with what organizations need and with the aspirations of the modern age. During a recent visit to Barcelona, I was bowled over again by the marvellous, uniquely creative work of Antoni Gaudi. Who can fail to be impressed by the vision and innovative concepts embodied by the cathedral, the Sagrada Familia? Conceived by Gaudi, this inspiring work is to be completed according to his plans by 2020, 100 years after his tragic death. You can visit Gaudi's studio and see a replica of a typical workshop where apprentices worked in a small team under the tutorship of a master craftsman. Gaudi ensured autonomy for the master and his small team in the execution of what would have seemed to be impossible ideas, which had, in many case, not been tried before. I was struck by the marriage of humanity and pragmatism in Gaudi's conviction that there is creative good in everyone, even nonconformists – one just has to discover where it is and conceive flexible ways for it to flourish. And this works when small groups trust each other in the pursuit of an inspiring goal. The idea that the organization should flex itself to bring out the best of the talent of individuals is applied by the most successful start-ups today – at least in the early stages – and also, as we will see, by some established enterprises. Why should we be surprised? There is nothing new under the sun!

Reinventing Organizations: A Guide to Creating Organizations Inspired by the Next Stage of Human Consciousness is the title of an important book by Frédéric Laloux, published in 2014 (Laloux, 2014). Laloux provides evidence of another high-performing model for organizing work that is out there. Laloux was driven to research and understand organizations that had applied a more dynamic and human approach to organizing work, to explore their performance as compared with their peer group, and to identify common features of how they worked that made them successful.

In his introduction, Laloux puts his inquiry into context: "… many people sense that the current way we run organizations has been stretched to its limits. We are increasingly disillusioned by organizational life. For people who toil away at the bottom of pyramids, surveys consistently report that work is more often than not dread and drudgery, not passion or purpose… And it's not only at the bottom of the pyramid. There is a dirty secret I have discovered in the 15 years I have spent consulting and coaching organizational leaders: life at the top of the pyramids isn't much more fulfilling. Behind the façade and bravado, the lives of powerful leaders are ones of quiet suffering too. Their frenetic activity is often a poor cover-up for a deep sense of emptiness. The power games, the politics, the infighting end up taking their toll on everybody…" Amen to that.

Laloux researches 12 "Evolutionary Teal" companies (a colour metaphor he applies compared with colours he uses for previous generations of organizational forms). We could also call these Digital Age Disruptive (DAD) structures. They are both representative of a new digital era – the Digital Age – and of the disruptive forces that established businesses face – disruptive.

The 12 organizations researched by Laloux have existed for many years, but in many ways they incarnate the working methods and process adopted by the best start-ups (new and not so new) that have disrupted and will disrupt established enterprises. The organizations profiled are both public and private, for-profit and not-for-profit, multinational (US, Netherlands, Germany and France, as well as global) and with 600 to 40,000 employees. All these organizations outperform their competitive peer groups, sometimes spectacularly.

Laloux identifies three breakthrough characteristics of these companies (*see Figure 7*):

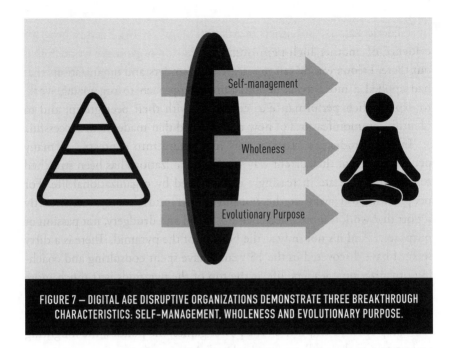

FIGURE 7 – DIGITAL AGE DISRUPTIVE ORGANIZATIONS DEMONSTRATE THREE BREAKTHROUGH CHARACTERISTICS: SELF-MANAGEMENT, WHOLENESS AND EVOLUTIONARY PURPOSE.

- **Self-management.** They operate effectively, even at scale, within a system based upon peer relationships, without the need for hierarchy or consensus.
- **Wholeness.** They create environments wherein employees are encouraged to bring their whole person to work, not just their rational selves. Employees do not park their emotional, intuitive and spiritual beings along with their cars when they arrive at work.
- **Evolutionary purpose.** Members of these organizations espouse the sense of purpose of the organization, where it wants to go and what it wants to achieve. The company becomes almost like a living organism with a purpose of its own, which employees, customers and other stakeholders latch on to. This is what drives the company forward. Financial results are a fortunate consequence, not a primary driver.

At first sight, you would think that this would be a recipe for anarchy! Interestingly, Laloux shows that these organizations have evolved rigorous practices and processes to harness these characteristics – just different!

It is not difficult to see how these characteristics appeal to the creative innovators of Generations X and Y, and why they are in many ways the default setting for how disruptive start-ups organize themselves – at least in the early years.

DISRUPTION LESSONS

There are important lessons to emerge from Laloux's work, and the examination of the rise and fall of the orthodox organization more generally, to carry forward into the rest of this book.

- First, nearly all the firms Laloux examined were organizations launched by a driven, usually charismatic, leader or small team (or in the case of family businesses, restarted by a new family member).
- Second, they thrived while they remained private under original leadership, but they reverted to conventional management approaches once they went public or came under new management. It follows that private (or at least non-public quoted) ownership was important for success.
- Third, unless both the CEO and the board "get it," there is no chance to make a successful transition toward a Digital Age, disruptive–type organization.
- Fourth, even if the leadership is on board, the raft of senior and middle managers below the executive suite will be the big resisters – they will lose both hierarchical power, and possibly even their jobs, as the logic of the new model plays out. After all, "Turkeys do not vote for Christmas."
- Fifth, a company transitioning from an orthodox organizational paradigm will never be able to achieve the costs, agility and dynamism of a "pure-play" Digital Age disruptive organization. Such is the overhang of legacy, including unionized labour and infrastructure that the journey is fraught with difficulty. "If I was going there, I would not start from here!"
- Sixth, organizations able to structure themselves along the Digital Age disruptive model will have a significant sustainable advantage. Whatever their intention, the effect of non-hierarchical, whole person, purpose-driven organizations will be to disrupt established business models, whether this was the intention or not.

These conclusions on orthodox organizations seem uncontroversial when I articulate them to senior executives. All seem to understand and agree, but such is the entrenched nature of denial in the psyche of the executive suite that ostrich-like behaviour often prevails. Why is this? Read on.

PART 2

DENIAL: HOW THIS SEEMS TO BE THE DEFAULT SETTING FOR ENTERPRISES WHEN CONFRONTED BY DISRUPTIVE CHANGE

CHAPTER 6
RECOGNIZING DENIAL

CHAPTER 6: RECOGNIZING DENIAL

Most people have had an experience of denial, small or large, in their lives. Can you remember being detached from the reality staring you in the face? Your irritation, even anger, when the evidence of reality intruded? Did you have a sense of unease in the background, but you carried on regardless?

Like many young couples, early in our marriage my wife and I had a yen to make our home in a historic building in a beautiful location – there were plenty of such opportunities back then in the southeast of England. We had little money, but big dreams! After many false starts, my wife bid at auction for the abandoned gymnasium of a bankrupt private school (itself a converted 17th century abbey) with splendid views over the Ashdown Forest – the inspiration for A.A. Milne's 100-acre wood in *Winnie the Pooh*. How more perfect could you get? Much to our surprise, she made the winning bid – right up to the limit of our budget! No worry, we thought, we had outline consent from the local government authority for the conversion we wanted to do and we would qualify for a grant for the building work, which would cover 25% of the budget.

A friendly, cooperative bank manager provided a bridging loan for the building works, the architect got building permission for our design, builders were selected and the project moved into full swing. The architect put in the application for the conversion grant – surely just a formality. Such a restoration met all the criteria. A few months later, the architect showed me a letter from the local government saying that our application for a grant had been reviewed by the relevant committee and refused. It explained that the grant was at their discretion, and that while the building met the criteria, we didn't qualify on the basis of financial need, given the price we had paid for the building and the development we were planning. *What idiots*, I remember thinking, *I will need to explain that we are impoverished young professionals, not developers! What a pain!* I wrote a long letter, explaining our situation and asking them to resubmit the application now that they were in full possession of the facts.

We carried on regardless; nothing changed. Even a further letter, saying that the chairman of the committee did not intend to resubmit our application to the next meeting, didn't alter our behaviour. As with all such projects, our ambitions expanded and costs overran, but we would tighten our belts. After all, the grant would come in once those idiot bureaucrats came to their senses. Or so I thought.

Months went by, the restoration advanced beautifully, the architect continued to give me certificates for me to make staged payments to the builders. Then there was no more money left for the next staged payment.

What a bore; I would have to go down to the local government offices 30 miles away and sort things out. And I was so busy! I remember just this sense of irritation to my busy life, not a need for contingency planning – but nevertheless, I had a sense of unease deep inside me, even as I carried on regardless. Weeks went by, nudges then demands for payment came from the builders, relayed by the architect.

It took an abortive trip to the local government offices, a frosty reception from an official, and an unpleasant meeting with the builder, who had been so friendly up to then, to force me to accept reality. We were not going to get the grant! Another trip to the bank manager would be needed. We hoped that he would be as friendly and cooperative as the previous time!

Of course, being a top executive, carrying on doing business-as-usual when there is evidence of disruption all around you is denial of a different order, you may be thinking. And I truly empathize as I think back to those events. Busy as ever, by temperament a doer, I was just frustrated by the intrusion of inconvenient, unplanned events, and carried on regardless.

Fortunately, in my little story the financial consequences were only embarrassing, not catastrophic. However, the experience was salutary. I like to think that my sense of entitlement, even hubris, diminished in later life. I took officialdom more seriously, and became more sympathetic to the frame of reference within which it must work.

THE NATURE OF DENIAL

Literature tells us that denial arises when a person is faced with a fact that is too uncomfortable to accept and rejects it instead, insisting that it's not true to the situation, despite overwhelming evidence to the contrary.

As I engage senior executives in conversation about the way digital technologies are threatening their business models, not to mention how the momentum for new styles of organizing work will encourage disruptive organizational forms, I come across behaviour very similar to this. Not all the time, of course, but very frequently.

Of course, denial expresses itself in various forms. It was the great psychoanalyst, Sigmund Freud, who first identified "Verneinung" (literally, the state of saying "no") as a psychological defence mechanism for patients unprepared to face facts that are too uncomfortable to accept. I do not, of course, suggest that senior individuals are in need of psychoanalysis at a personal level, but there is no denying that what I see is denial! So perhaps they do need a form of psychoanalysis at a collegiate and corporate level!

The literature also tells us that a person may adopt three basic types of denial:

- Simple denial: denying the reality of the unpleasant fact altogether.
- Minimization: admitting the fact but denying its seriousness (a combination of denial and rationalization).
- Projection: admitting both the fact and its seriousness but denying responsibility by blaming somebody or something else.

I personally have not come across senior people who flat out reject the disruption we are talking about. There may well be, of course, disruption deniers in the same way as there are Holocaust deniers or climate change deniers, but I have not seen such behaviour at a top management level. However, I suggest that the second two types of denial are widespread across incumbent businesses, indeed are often the norm.

Here are a few attitudes I have heard recently:

"It's a fad, and it will go away."

"We must not get distracted as we all were in the dot-com boom or with Y2K."

"Disruption will not affect our clients or business model – disruptors will just play in the low end."

"It will take years for there to be any impact."

"We must stick to our knitting, complete our digital transformation programme and get on with it."

"There is no way that any new player could ever dislodge our brands."

"Good luck with the massive investment they will need!"

HOW THE EXECUTIVE BRAIN FUNCTIONS – LESSONS FROM NEUROSCIENCE

Before being too hard on our corporate deniers, I have been trying to understand how the relevant parts of the brain work, to explore if there is something about this that determines how we breed senior managers, and whether this can explain denial behaviour.

It appears that denial is a natural consequence of how senior executives' brains work and how they have learned to exercise them over the years. In fact, denial is the natural default setting!

Here is my simplified layman's understanding of the brain and how it might influence denial.

One widely used model for looking at the brain is the concept of left brain and right brain functions. Cognitive functions, such as analysis, rational reasoning, logic and calculation, come from in the left brain – distinct from the creative, emotional and intuitive functions in the right brain. Both these "brains" come into play in influencing denial in executives confronted by threatening forces (*see Figure 8*).

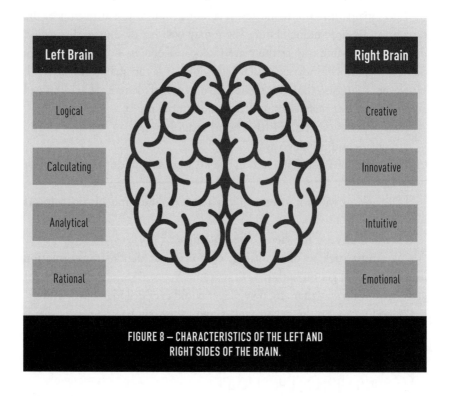

Left Brain

Logical

Calculating

Analytical

Rational

Right Brain

Creative

Innovative

Intuitive

Emotional

FIGURE 8 – CHARACTERISTICS OF THE LEFT AND RIGHT SIDES OF THE BRAIN.

COGNITION

On top of our physical brains is the cerebral cortex, or what some call the "human brain" (as distinct from our "lizard" and "mammalian" brains, products of the earlier stages of evolution). Complex electrical circuits fire and switch off as the cortex connects with deeper areas of the brain. The cerebral cortex was the last part of the human brain to evolve and the most complex and sophisticated – and it is evolving all the time. It is responsible for decision-making and cognitive logic.

Cognitive left brain functions constitute our ability to work in a meaningful way with information gathered from all our senses. We match new information with information we have gained previously and memorized, apply our preferences and, as necessary, change our opinions based upon this information and process.

In management, good cognitive brain functions are vital – a person can quickly relate complex information to previous knowledge and turn this to an advantage. This is a reasoned (rather than intuitive) process.

Research in both the workplace and within psychotherapy demonstrates that cognitive performance is closely linked to mood and state of health. Although some can seem to cope well up to a burnout point, in reality, cognitive performance can fall off the cliff when a person is stressed or depressed, for example. By contrast, cognitive performance is able to flourish when the individual feels safe, loved and affirmed.

Sadly, stress is a frequent state for top executives, which in extreme cases can lead to burnout. The hierarchical, command and control nature of the orthodox organizational form encourages feelings that diminish cognitive performance – deadlines, self-justification, competition from colleagues, and performance measurement, among others. The highest levels of cognitive performance will only occur when the executive is working with empathetic colleagues in a stress-free environment. Rare indeed!

INNOVATION

The human brain is masterful in recognizing things that are out of the norm. This helped with survival – when we saw something odd, the orbital frontal cortex was stimulated and sent a direct message to the fear centres of the brain in the amygdala. "Hey, be careful, watch out, this is dangerous!" This is the dominant learned pattern of our brain.

This does not help with developing curiosity and innovation. This default setting can be rewired, but with difficulty – by exposure to new ideas or by testing out new ideas in a stress-free environment, for example.

Rewiring the brain toward embracing right brain innovation functions requires decluttering and focus. This is why the most productive people in white coats in labs have been set free to focus on their research science, and do not have myriad other things to do – not to mention meetings to attend, turf wars to fight, bureaucratic administrations to deal with and so on. Unfortunately, senior executives' available time for productive thinking and creativity is compromised by much clutter!

INSTINCT

The brain has a remarkable capacity to recognize patterns, process data and cause us to make instantaneous decisions without thinking about it. When we cross the road, our left cognitive brain helps us process the height of the pavement, the light, the presence and speed of traffic, the distance to be crossed, how out of breath we feel and so on. But this learned experience can also process data to trigger an instinctive response – instinct that the traffic lights are about to change or that a speeding car is about to come around the corner – and we adapt our behaviour accordingly.

The area that enables intuition is also in the right side of the brain. Here is where creative thought, artistic and musical flair, senses and emotion are generated – and it is now acknowledged that the cortex also plays a part in intuition. Neuroscientists believe that intuitive capacity is domain-specific – i.e., one can have good insight in one domain, but have lousy instinct in another. And the more familiar you are with a domain, the faster the brain processes instantaneous solutions. In other words, practice makes perfect. This is obvious in sports, when a good team player knows instinctively where the ball will be passed– as much by instinct as anything else.

My wife and I like to watch professional tennis, both live and on TV. I amuse my family and friends by sometimes calling out "double fault" just as a server has tossed the ball up for a second service. And I surprise myself, and them, by how often I am right. What is going on here? In my teens and early 20s, I was not a bad tennis player – not a professional, of course, but I used to play at a competitive league level with some success. I suggest that my experience of how the ball has been tossed, the player's body position, my perception of the body language of the player, the tension in the air and so on, allow my brain to see recurring patterns and propose an outcome for the second service situation – instantaneously without recourse to the conscious cognitive networks of the brain.

Malcolm Gladwell's book, *Blink* (Gladwell, 2006), has had a big influence on the trading floors of financial institutions. He makes the case for the power and effectiveness of instinct, gut feel and snap judgements – particularly when exercised by highly experienced people and when those people are empowered to feel that they can use their intuition.

The reality is that most established scientific rationalist organizations are horrified by "gut feel" and any decision-making based upon pure intuition. They need data, analysis and rational deduction as a basis of decision-making. And experience, which is the precondition for effective intuition, is also undervalued. As soon as someone is good at something, we promote him or her to something else. The experience of practitioners may be taken into account, but decision-making that matters is taken elsewhere in the organization (by the "HiPPO" – the highest-paid person's opinion – see chapter 2). So when senior executives have an intuition based upon experience that something is seriously wrong – for example, the imminence of disruption – they are trained to distrust and repress this feeling. They therefore underuse the capacity of the human brain – what a waste! What frustration!

BEHAVIOURAL BIASES AT WORK

I have been interested in exploring further if there are other aspects of the brain's behaviours that explain or encourage the states of denial we have been exploring.

PATTERN RECOGNITION BIAS

The cognitive brain has an incredibly sophisticated capability to remember patterns that it has observed before. In fact, this pattern-recognition capability lies at the heart of parenting, learning, training and surviving in the world. We learn to feel comfortable with patterns of behaviour we have seen and adopted before. We love working with familiar patterns. We tend to stick to things we know well. As a consequence, the brain has a tendency to reject anything disruptive to established patterns.

So if we want leaders with a bias toward dealing with disruption, we need perhaps to look in places where different patterns are established, ones where the brain sees change and threat as commonplace. Perhaps the effective leaders for a disruptive world will come from outside the usual contexts of business. We will explore this further in the next chapter.

CONFIRMATION BIAS

When threatened, the brain tends to scan for facts and circumstances that confirm the lens through which its owner sees the world. Selecting these facts will comfort the person in his or her established view. This natural bias is intensified by the abrupt increase in the availability of data, which snowballs, as the Big Data phenomenon discussed earlier shows. There is much more data and authoritative research available for us to select and to confirm our view of the world.

We need to acknowledge that questioning the status quo is not a characteristic valued by the recruiters of top managers. Their mission is to scan for candidates who conform to the established view of the world.

RELATIONSHIP BIAS

The brain learns that its owner wants to be liked. People wish to please others. Most people do not want to offend, create a fuss or disagree publicly with peers. Supportive interpersonal relationships are valued and disruptive behaviour is distrusted. A board member of an important public body told me this story:

"There was an important investment about to be nodded through. Just before the vote, I piped up diffidently with another point of view. Very soon, others expressed unhappiness with what was being proposed and supported my view. Before long, everyone was on board, and we ended up deciding something completely different than what was originally proposed. The danger of not wanting to rock the boat! I see it all the time."

Incumbent organizations have powerful immune systems capable of rejecting disruptive foreign bodies!

CONCLUSIONS ON DENIAL

Let us not beat ourselves up about denial. It is a natural state, given who we are and where we sit if we find ourselves in a senior position in an established enterprise.

Take on board the reality that the working environment of most senior executives suppresses cognitive performance (good decision-making); that anything new is perceived as a threat and is to be distrusted; and that gut-feel based upon learned experience is considered dangerous.

So when facing an existential threat from disruption, what is the default setting of the brain of a senior executive? Something that looks very like denial:

- "I can't get my mind around it because I am too stressed."
- "This new thing is threatening; I should reject it."
- "I shouldn't trust my intuition and the feeling of disquiet in my gut that this is something really important."

Recognize the biases that are built up inside organizations; we tend to reproduce patterns of what has worked in the past, or what is considered acceptable. We are in danger of selecting data that support our received view or prejudice – and there is more and more data available for us to select. Few of us want to "rock the boat" and put company relationships at risk by taking contrarian views.

If your company is doing well, results are good and stock market analysts are scoring you well, this is when denial is likely to be most prevalent. After all, "If it works, don't fix it!" If short-term results are good, your board is unlikely to be enthusiastic about initiatives to confront disruptive threats, particularly if measures compromise short-term performance – and particularly if the executive team is less than enthusiastic.

Trust the sense of unease you might feel when you sense that your company is complacent or if it wants to "carry on regardless." This is the stirring of acceptance, a precondition of moving beyond denial, of dealing with the disruptive world, and the first step toward survival and prosperity in this new world. We look at this in more detail in chapter 9.

CHAPTER 7
INBREEDING SYNDROME

Most of us know that if a species breeds within a restricted family circle, then negative physiological and psychological consequences and weaknesses can be introduced to the gene pool. In fact, our ancestors recognized the dangers of inbreeding by establishing laws on marriage, banning intermarriage and therefore discouraging reproduction within the close family.

I spent much of my childhood in Africa and was able to make frequent visits to remote areas and game parks. I learned that animals of the savannah thrived in their natural habitats when established rules, hierarchies and breeding rituals have been respected. In a recent wildlife documentary, David Attenborough (The Hunt, 2015) described the enforced inbreeding of cheetahs as their environment changes. These magnificent animals have been used to living on home ranges, which average 2,000-sq. km – they need their space. However, as the human population has expanded, many of the traditional habitats of the cheetah have been destroyed or become fragmented. Cheetahs cannot find mates outside their close family group. The increased forced rates of inbreeding give rise to more infectious diseases, poor sperm quality and dental anomalies, such as focal palatine erosion. Surely, this is also true in the business world – genetic diversity is vital to an organization's ability to evolve productively and adapt to disruption in its environment. Low levels of genetic diversity can be fatal!

THE TOP MANAGEMENT BREED – WHAT IT IS AND WHERE IT COMES FROM

Earlier I told the story of how I was contacted by an executive search recruiter with an attractive job proposition. Two years after leaving INSEAD with my MBA, I was then working in a middle-management position at Esso in the UK. Apparently I had been identified as a serious candidate for the CEO position of a division of a well-known, mid-sized industrial conglomerate. I was flabbergasted! Of course, I was flattered! Probably fortunately for all concerned, I did not pursue the opportunity – I had neither knowledge nor interest in the industry concerned. Nor did I feel remotely capable, let alone ready, for such a role.

I can imagine the process that was followed by the recruiter as he checked off my profile against the specifications that had been agreed with the client. Age – early thirties. Check. Education – good first degree, plus an MBA from a top school. Check. Ten-years plus in a premium industrial enterprise (I had had 9 jobs in 11 years at Esso). Check. Experience in a range of functional areas, plus some line-management experience. Check. Languages – French and/or German. Check. References – on the fast track, good interpersonal skills and liked by his colleagues. Check.

I was, indeed, an ideal candidate, it would appear!

It may be that, in those days, the search for senior executives was less sophisticated than it is today. There was little or no psychometric or personality testing then, although I am not sure how widespread, nor useful, these methods are even now. When I look at the size, scope and apparent sophistication of the human resources departments of large enterprises, not to mention the cost, surely things must have improved!

A survey from the executive search firm Heidrick and Struggles, available on their website (Heidrick & Struggles, 2015), shows that nearly all CEOs have university degrees and 24% of them in the UK are educated at the elite Oxford and Cambridge Universities. In France, the situation is even more pronounced – 92% of CEOs hold post-graduate degrees from elite schools. The situation is similar in the US and other developed industrial economies. So we can assume that our top people are at least partially products of their educational system. It seems that recruitment of senior executives draws from the gene pool of a high management caste, trained in elite universities and topped up in the "science" of management at top business schools. These people are deployed either as executives or as consultants to drive businesses about which they may have little first-hand knowledge nor apprenticeship. It is they who define the strategy, secure the resources, and put in place the processes, systems and controls that are meant to ensure that plans are executed as intended. They oversee the development of the infrastructure, systems and processes required to deal with a rapidly changing, more complex world.

In a world where denial is the default setting for executives at the top of established enterprises, when confronted with existential disruptive change, is it likely that you will change much by this approach? Does inbreeding not perpetuate the phenomenon of denial and institutional stasis?

A RARE NEW BREED – PRODUCTIVE DISRUPTORS

It is possible to recruit people who are different, determined to be productive and creative, and to fight the bureaucracy of the "managerialistic" system that enfolds them. They do exist, but they are difficult to find.

One of the most prestigious executive search firms, Russell Reynolds, offers some evidence of this in a 2015 article, available on their website, entitled "What Differentiates the Top Digital Executives: The Emergence of Productive Disruptors" (Russell Reynolds, 2015). (*See Figure 9.*)

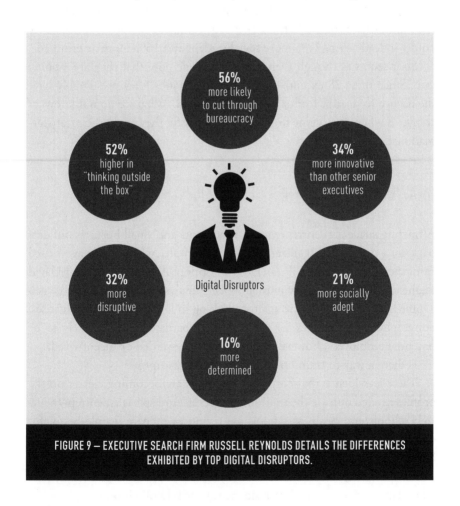

FIGURE 9 – EXECUTIVE SEARCH FIRM RUSSELL REYNOLDS DETAILS THE DIFFERENCES EXHIBITED BY TOP DIGITAL DISRUPTORS.

They conducted psychometric assessments and qualitative interviews with 28 of the world's top "digital executives" (responsible for digital transformation initiatives), whom they characterized as "productive disruptors." They found that these executives were 56% more likely to cut through bureaucracy than the broader population of senior leaders. They also scored 52% higher in "thinking outside the box."

"These leaders do aim to disrupt – they leverage their interpersonal skills to productively disrupt. They not only see the future and understand how to get there, they energize their colleagues to take the journey with them," says the Russell Reynolds report. These digital transformation leaders are 34% more innovative than other senior executives, 32% more disruptive, 23% bolder in leadership, 21% more socially adept and 16% more determined.

So it seems as though there is another gene pool that they are tapping into. Since these 28 executives are still in their jobs, they presumably have the licence to disrupt from a CEO who "gets it." What we do not know, of course, is where they came from or how successful they are in their transformational endeavours.

DRAWING FROM ANOTHER GENE POOL?

Attracting successful entrepreneurs, innovators and small business builders back into orthodox organizations – for example, when they have exited from their businesses – will rarely be an option. As Jason Fried and David Heinemeier Hansson show in their *Rework* analysis (Hansson, 2010), such people actively discriminate against working in large orthodox enterprises. Some may be candidates for positions on boards, but are unlikely to be potential employees, however highly they are rewarded or incentivized.

Is there a way to train up your own senior disruptors?

There is evidence that corporate recruiters are becoming clearer on the profiles needed outside the traditional process. And specialist entrepreneurship schools and business schools are trying to prepare people better for entrepreneurship – not just "start-your-own-business" entrepreneurship, but also corporate entrepreneurship. It is great to see, for example, that my own alma mater, INSEAD, now has the master of platforms, Sangeet Paul Choudary, as entrepreneur-in-residence at the school. Hooray!

CHAPTER 8

THE "STUCKNESS PREDICAMENT"

We have seen how the way the brain is conditioned by our background, the way business is done, and the inbreeding of senior executives in the organization mean that the natural default setting for top executives in confronting disruptive change is denial. And inbreeding conspires to standardize attitudes and perpetuate denial.

Top executives can also feel powerless to do much – they are trapped in the system. "So why bother?" I call this the "Stuckness Predicament" (*see Figure 10*).

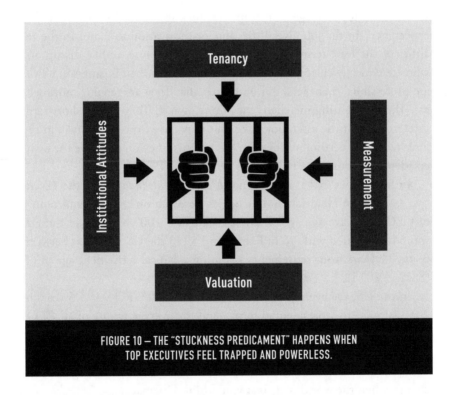

FIGURE 10 – THE "STUCKNESS PREDICAMENT" HAPPENS WHEN TOP EXECUTIVES FEEL TRAPPED AND POWERLESS.

Most of the "stuckness" that senior executives and boards feel about responding to disruptive change derives from being subject to the rules and constraints of the shareholder capital system. The articles of incorporation of all public enterprises (with some slight variations by country jurisdiction) place the fiduciary responsibility on boards of directors to look after the interests of shareholders, the owners of the corporation. The board must ensure that the CEO and management team deliver short-term results in line with expectations, while at the same time ensuring the long-term health of the business.

In practice, executive teams are caught in four traps that preclude them from taking a long-term view and from responding proactively to disruption, even when this is clear and inevitable.

THE TENANCY TRAP

A CEO and top management team are stuck in the reality that their "life expectancy" in the job gives little time or motivation to factor in the realities of the long-term into their plans. Furthermore, unlike disruptors, who are typically entrepreneurs who start and own their businesses, CEOs are professional managers, not entrepreneurs. They are tenants, not owners. They are renting the chair; they don't own it. They have a short-term interest in what the asset looks like, but may have little or no stake in the long-term appreciation of the asset. As tenants, they do not have the owners' depth of commitment.

In September 2015, the journal *Management Today* cited the executive search firm Heidrich and Struggles' research on the ages and tenure of CEOs. The average age of a boss of a FTSE 100 company in the UK was 54, compared with 56 in France and 59 in the US. This was between 6 and 11 years from retirement, assuming a typical retirement age of 65 (Savage, 2015).

In the US, the average tenure of a Fortune 500 CEO was 4.6 years in 2013 (similar to a presidential term), and the average tenure of all CEOs was 8.1 years. So, as any President of the USA will tell you, this is not much time to be able to demonstrate the fruits of innovative change! And it requires a particularly determined character to force through radical change when the world is against you! Think Obamacare!

The 4.6-year length of the average CEO tenure means that he or she is almost literally here today, gone tomorrow. So the CEO is going to make sure that whatever he or she does in the first year or two achieves a measurable result in year four, in time for the CV to be updated and impress headhunters for the next opportunity. Disruption is perceived to be so uncertain, so distant and, above all, so potentially upsetting to customers that it does not feature in the five-year horizon or objectives of a CEO.

THE MEASUREMENT TRAP

There is an old saw in management: "Measurement predicates behaviour." CEOs and top management teams are under enormous pressure from boards, analysts and shareholders to achieve satisfactory results in the short-term – every quarter in the case of a US-quoted company, every six months in the UK. This forces management to live from day to day. They have little or no incentive to fight this pressure, given their short-term tenure and tenancy status.

Typically, a CEO's performance is measured by, and remuneration incentivized against, largely short-term measures: Key Performance Indicators (KPIs) such as revenue targets, profitability measures, return on shareholders' capital and perhaps measures of employee engagement. Measures to incentivize longer-term performance, such as stock options with delayed vesting periods, are becoming widely applied – but mainly to mitigate the perception of excessive executive pay rather than to act as a strong incentive to long-term performance. One senior executive put it to me this way: "It's a bit like asking your partner to lay the chips on the roulette table – you have little influence in the result, but there is a chance you might win!"

So, there is little wonder that typical CEOs are stuck when it comes to making fundamental changes. They can feel trapped within the "system." They may know that they should be doing things to ensure the long-term health (even survival) of the business – but this gets pushed to the back of their minds by the pressure of the performance environment. Their freedom to act is prescribed and their incentives push them in a different direction.

- "I have little mind space for the longer-term – next quarter results must be my focus."
- "My board is interested in presentations about the future, but the nitty gritty is earnings and share price."
- "My bonus is linked to results, not dreams."
- "I will deliver on my mandate. When I am gone, let the next guy deal with it."

THE VALUATION TRAP

As taught in business literature and business schools, the CEO's primary task is to maximize the shareholder value of the enterprise. The normal formula to quantify this is to calculate the present value of projected future cash flows. The discount rate applied to the future cash flows depends upon the risk premium (up or down) a shareholder applies to reflect the risk of the plans to deliver those cash flows – for example, from presence in fragile markets, exposure to unionized labour, risk of regulatory intervention, and exposure to litigation from unforeseen accidents, among others. If the Discounted Cash Flow (DCF) return adjusted for risk is greater than the rate at which the enterprise can borrow on the capital markets (the opportunity cost of capital), then making the investment will enhance the value of the enterprise, so the investment should be made. And of course, if lower, then it should not be pursued.

This analytical framework of Shareholder Value Maximization (SVM) applies to all assessments of value creation in an enterprise – investment proposals, acquisitions, restructuring, even valuation of the enterprise itself (although in practice, the share price reflects markets' perceptions of value and potential, rather than any obvious linkage to discounted cash flows). The problem with the valuation trap is in its execution, not in its intent. The organization may play lip service to long-term shareholder value objectives through the deployment of a DCF analysis, which can look in great detail at the market, market share, pricing and costing assumptions in years one through three, but the final investment decision often relies on standard formulas applied by rote or even by applying an automated formula for terminal value, often computed in year five. Furthermore, decision-making is dominated by "getting the numbers right."

My very first encounter with the mysteries and quirkiness of Discounted Cash Flow proved to be my first grasp of the slippery pole of career progression. As a young sales representative with Esso in the UK, I had negotiated the chance for Esso to acquire an independently owned petrol filling station on the outskirts of a country town in the south of England. I was to present the business case to the retail investment committee in person – me a young shaver with little experience. I slaved away to prepare some photos and storyboards showing sales potential and threats from competition, and drew up a list of assumptions for the business case. Having studied up on DCF and investigated hurdle rates and norms applied by the committee for agreeing acquisitions, I sent off the input forms to head office IT for them to run the various scenarios I suggested. Not to my surprise, the DCF for the base case was marginal at best and unlikely to meet the hurdle rate for what was a quite risky opportunity. But we carried on regardless, and there I was in front of these illustrious elders making my presentation. It went surprisingly well. They liked my story and how it was presented (I learned that a slick presentation can cover up a multitude of sins!) and they seemed to want to do it. There then ensued a long and what appeared to me esoteric conversation about terminal values and hurdle rates. My 20-year cash flow had included a disposal value in year 20 of twice the current alternative use value of the site – someone had told me that this was the metric to use. Apparently, we could use a terminal value multiple of three, not two, given the residential expansion that would take place around the service station. The competitive intensity was low, therefore the risk premium was lower, so we could use a lower discount rate, they reckoned. Rerunning the numbers on this basis showed that the project met the criteria and the project was agreed upon.

Even in those days, a much more stable world when 20-year cash flows and pricing assumptions made some kind of sense, managers had to make the numbers work. In a sense, they were slaves to the analytical tool. They were stuck – they thought the investment made sense, but could not justify making it unless the numbers said okay. This is not meant as a criticism of the Esso managers, just a reality. In fact, the acquisition turned about to be okay – not brilliant, but okay.

Things have changed over the years. The world has become less stable, less predictable, and cash-flow forecasts also reflect this. But managers are still stuck unless they can make the numbers work. In most established companies, cash flows are now done over shorter periods focusing on early year cash flows, and little attention is paid to terminal values. The nature of discounted cash flows is such that the more accurately predictable cash flows from the early years carry greater weight than cash flows delivered from longer-term strategic moves, such as technology, geographical mix or bets on innovation in products or services.

In reality, the correct pursuit of SVM should force managers to make investment decisions that fully take into account the long term. Scenario analysis, strategy development and financial forecasting inherent in DCF analysis, the mechanism for SVM, if done properly, should serve as a spur to tackling potential disruption. No CEO could report to his board that the next five years look great but things might start to look a bit dodgy and disruptive in year eight and get away with it.

However, from my experience, the problem is that CEOs and top management teams do not pursue SVM correctly, and boards let them get away with it. Instead, they prepare strategic plans with three- or five-year horizons, showing healthy growth in revenues and EBITDA, and promising payback on capital investment plans, but without any significant analysis of what the company will look like in year five and beyond. The return is highly dependent upon the terminal values, often easily stated but difficult if not impossible to justify in a disruptive world. Terminal values are applied willy nilly, without any serious thought as to whether the final year cash flow, often in year five, is conceivably sustainable ad infinitum.

When boards allow the slavish application of DCF analysis in this fashion to justify investment and innovation, they are complicit in short-termism and the effective denial of disruptive forces of which they may be aware but that are "over the horizon." They are not fulfilling their fiduciary duty of overseeing the long-term sustainable health and value of the enterprise. While executives have excuses for denial, boards do not.

Private equity firms look at things differently. They have to look at what the firm will look like in year five, because that is when they will be exiting. So a three- to five-year forecast of financials is only part one of the story. Equally important is the strategic position of the target in year five, which is what will determine future value, their exit value. They recognize the dangers of DCF and rarely think about investment purely in this way.

THE INSTITUTIONAL ATTITUDES TRAP

I am indebted to my friend, Professor John Shotter, for pointing me toward the analytical philosophers Ludwig Wittgenstein and Gabriel Stolzenberg to provide a basis in philosophy and psychology for the Stuckness Predicament.

When individuals are immersed in the traditions, attitudes and practices of a strong "social community," they embody the language, attitudes and practices of that community. In a sense, the social community and the individual become one, at least when they are active in that social community. Not, of course, when they are elsewhere – at home, for instance. Wittgenstein describes the "stare and gape" of an intelligent individual hearing challenges to the orthodoxy of the social community.

In his inquiry into the foundations of mathematics, Stolzenberg describes the process of entrapment: "*The process of entrapment.* Insofar as its general form is concerned, it consists, first, *in being taken in* by certain uses of language that have the appearance, but only that, of being meaningful; and by certain modes of reasoning that have the appearance, but only that, of being self-evidently correct; second, *in being locked in* as a result of the psychological act, or process, to accepting these appearances as being "really so." Somehow, by a process that may be quite complex, they become so thoroughly woven into the very fabric of what we take to be our web of reality that it no longer seems possible to adopt a standpoint from which the question of their correctness may be entertained seriously as a "mere" hypothesis. What were, originally, assumptions have now become givens and the idea of calling them into question is no longer intelligible" (Stolzenberg, 1978).

In other words, the "web of reality" of top executives is conditioned by the way of doing things and attitudes expressed by colleagues and board members. It becomes virtually impossible to challenge widely embedded orthodoxy baked into how the organization behaves, prioritizes and communicates. Any moves toward dealing with existential threats or initiatives toward disruptive innovations to the existing business model or value network cannot be taken seriously. They are stuck!

POWERLESS IN THE FACE OF DISRUPTIVE INNOVATION

This reality of being stuck in the "system" and not taking disruptive innovation threats seriously is picked up by Clayton Christiansen in his seminal work, *The Innovator's Dilemma: When New Technologies Cause Great Firms to Fail* (Christensen, 1997). As we discovered in chapter 1, Christiansen challenged the established orthodoxy that business failures are due to bad managers not keeping up with technology. He showed that well-managed firms are usually aware of the new technological innovations. But the way they do business does not allow them to pursue disruptive innovations when they arise. These are not profitable enough at first. The way firms plan, value investment proposals, and allocate resources stops them from pursuing radical innovations, either because the numbers will not work, or because it would take scarce resources away from sustaining innovations in products and services to existing customers, which are needed to compete against current rivals.

I would add, from my experience, that the gating processes traditionally applied to projects, from inception to execution, mean that there are great ideas that never see the light of day because they are filtered through layers of management review and screened against crude measures such as DCF, which do not adequately take account of existential threats.

On the other hand, Christiansen shows, start-ups have different business models and value networks. They can use the new technology to deliver value to customers in different ways, usually at significantly lower cost. Incumbents leave the start-ups freedom to operate since they are incapable of responding.

Christiansen defines value networks as "The collection of upstream suppliers, downstream channels to market, and ancillary providers that support a common business model within the industry." In other words, the established order for doing business in that industry. Successful disruptive start-ups choose to disrupt these established value networks. If they conform to the established order, they fail. "When would-be disruptors enter into existing value networks, they must adapt their business models to conform to the value networks and therefore fail that disruption because they become co-opted."

Initially, start-ups apply different value networks and are largely ignored by incumbents. But it is not long before they are able to invade the older value networks, and with a significantly better-performing business model. At that point, the established firm in that old value network is condemned to fend off the attack on its market share. Thereafter, managing for survival (rather than thriving) becomes the order of the day.

CONCLUSIONS ON THE STUCKNESS PREDICAMENT

I find widespread resignation within top teams about their Stuckness Predicament – almost ennui. "Que sera, sera."

The shareholder capitalistic model of the enterprise conspires so that senior executives in established organizations focus on incremental, rather than fundamental, disruptive change: short-term results must not be compromised; incentives and rewards are rarely aligned with longer-term strategic imperatives. The "life expectancy" of top executives tends to make them focus on incrementalism; and analysis methods promote short-term performance rather than long-term threats. Most boards are conditioned not to rock the boat.

The ambience and culture of many organizations seems to encourage inertia – it is so difficult to get things done. This can provoke a sense of fatalism in many top executives. As one put it to me: "We can never change fast enough; let my successor deal with it!"

Senior executives in established enterprises can feel stuck, because the institution takes on a mind of its own, and it seems impossible to shake it into a different direction. The organization takes on a web of perceived reality, which is woven into the very fabric of the enterprise; assumptions cannot be questioned and have now become givens, and the idea of calling them into question is no longer intelligible to colleagues.

In the face of disruptive change from new competitors and business models, senior executives feel powerless to respond. They feel stuck in the reality of their own business model and value networks, and rationalize to themselves that the new competitor is unthreatening, even when it begins to affect the company's own business model and value networks.

In short, the Stuckness Predicament reinforces denial. In the next chapter, we explore how to move to a state of acceptance, a precondition for shaking off stuckness and for survival in the disruptive world.

PART 3

MOVING BEYOND DENIAL: OBLIGATIONS AND OPTIONS FOR SURVIVAL

CHAPTER 9

REACHING A STATE OF ACCEPTANCE

AVOID BEING A DENIAL DENIER

Before dismissing disruption and denial as real and present dangers (being a denial denier!), consider the following.

Most enterprises are set up to deal with forces of instability, which affect their traditional business model and value networks – both the "knowns" and the "known unknowns" – such as the rise and fall of emerging markets, globalization, the squeeze on resources and many other factors that figure in scenario planning within their orthodox approach to business. They can respond, innovate and adapt to these threats.

Things get a bit more problematic when they consider longer-term existential threats, which in due course are likely to catch companies unawares – climate change, depletion of resources due to population growth, and fundamentalist terrorism, for example. After all, we have evidence of how business and political leaders appeared blindsided by short-term instabilities staring them in the face; they were fully aware of the unsustainable factors that led to the financial crash of 2007-2008. Yet the whole world appeared to have been caught unawares! How much more so, surely, for longer-term existential threats "over the horizon."

In his speech to the insurers at Lloyd's of London in September 2015, Mark Carney, the governor of the Bank of England, talked of the "Tragedy of Horizons" with respect to climate change: the chronic inability of business and political leaders to tackle challenges beyond their short-term horizon. "It presents an existential threat to the status quo," yet hardly figures in day-to-day operational planning. "It's too big, too scary and, most of all, too distant to start planning for" and "… once climate change becomes a defining issue for financial stability, it may already be too late." (Carney, 2015). And this was a serious threat for the insurance of physical assets. In other words, denial.

Many will dismiss reflections such as Carney's as those of a prophet of doom with no recognition of the power of the human spirit, free enterprise and technology to tackle and deal with climate change head-on. Assuming you are not a climate change denier, do you really feel comfortable about this?

The disruptive threats discussed in this book are not "over the horizon" – they are real and immediate. Their scale, scope, reach and pace of adoption are pretty clear. Answer frankly if you think that your business is set up to acknowledge and deal with what may prove to be existential threats to the business, which we have been exploring:

- The disruptive innovation to established business models and value networks of start-ups and digital businesses, combined with the inability of well-managed established enterprises to respond
- The new ways of thinking and behaving of digital natives
- The fundamental shift from "pipes" to "platforms" with the customer at the centre of the ecosystem
- The emergence of new ways of organizing work, which make orthodox hierarchies and command and control processes appear ineffective by comparison.

THE JOURNEY TO ACCEPTANCE

In business, as in psychotherapy, the first step for moving on from denial is acceptance. This requires both the board and executive management team to accept the reality and its seriousness, and their responsibility for doing something about it.

To be clear, we are talking about acceptance of the inevitability of disruption and the need to consider radical response strategies, not just the need to "get serious about digital." Acceptance does not mean kidding ourselves. Market analysts are keen to see that companies are indeed "going digital" – digital transformation programmes of various sorts abound, including digitization, "digital first," personalization, curated websites, robotics, multichannel, omnichannel, Big Data and analytics. Acceptance requires a recognition of a need for something much more fundamental.

As demonstrated in part 2 of this book, there are obstacles to reaching a genuine state of acceptance – the way top executives think and the biases that influence them, the obligations and realities of working within a shareholder-driven capitalistic environment (the Stuckness Predicament) and the institutional focus on incremental innovation at the expense of disruptive innovation, for example.

So how do you know when a state of acceptance has been attained? This requires both admission of the fact and the desire to do something about it.

For some corporations, reaching a state of acceptance of the threat is easy – but setting a course to doing something about it less so. The president and CEO of a well-known global drinks company recently put it to me this way: "At board and executive-team levels, we all see it. Customers see our brands as lifestyle choices, part of a network of products and services shared with friends online. Their reflex is to listen to their friends and to buy online at Amazon and other online supermarkets, and before long they will be doing so. We do not sell to customers direct and dare not do so because we depend on drinks wholesalers, which own rights to sales and distribution in their territories. Their commissions kill us, but our people dare not build brand, sales and relationships directly with customers, fearing retaliation. We are damned if we do, and we are damned if we don't! Middle managers in their 50s resist change at all costs – getting them to think survival and disruption is a challenge!" In this case, the reality of the situation was fully acknowledged (the unsustainability over the long-term of the status quo) and the major obstacle to change known (the intransigence of middle managers in their 50s), but what would it take to embark upon the fundamental changes needed?

I recently made a visit to the production plant of a respected precision engineering company in a provincial French town, in the company of a soon-to-retire executive director. On the way, he insisted that there was no way his company was threatened by disruption. They were a well-established and respected manufacturer of industrial valves, with a profitable niche in the manufacture of these parts for bulk Liquid Natural Gas (LNG) carrier tankers, where engineering excellence in cryogenics, mastery of precision tolerances, compliance to industry standards and reputation were everything. Indeed, as we walked around the plant, a group of Koreans was examining the manufacture of valves for the tankers that would be delivering gas to them. They wanted to refine specifications to the ship owners and operators who would be building new ships.

A while later, over a long lunch, we discussed where disruptive change might come from. It was becoming clear that traditional materials and practices in the safe handling of gases under high pressure at low temperatures (cryogenics) were being rethought – by the company itself, in the labs of the University of Limoges, and by some small companies experimenting with new materials and methods. In-line sensors and algorithmic analysis were opening up new possibilities in materials science – stainless steel, carbon fibre, pressure seals and sealants. And production methods were changing. It was difficult to keep up – robotics and remote manufacture using 3D printing techniques. The safety inspection agencies, on whom they were highly dependent for approvals and compliance, were considering listing alternative product designs and materials that the company was not well set up to respond to. As a supplier of specialty parts, it was highly dependent on the established value networks – national gas buyers, ship owners, construction yards, and gas terminal operators in gas-producing countries. The company was vulnerable link in a delicate chain. My friend admitted that most of this was well known inside the company, but there was an atmosphere of resignation – "carry on regardless." What would it take to be prepared to get going with fundamental change? A state of acceptance, as opposed to resignation, combined with the determination to do something fundamental about it, perhaps.

NO INDUSTRY IS IMMUNE TO DISRUPTION AND DENIAL

It is important to reflect on and accept the idea that no industry is immune from disruption. The examples below illustrate how even those industries that require significant capital to enter cannot escape. And some significant players are reaching a state of acceptance that disruptive change is possible.

NO INDUSTRY IS IMMUNE FROM FUNDAMENTAL DISRUPTION

As we saw earlier, Michael Porter's "Barriers to Entry" doctrine points out that industries are attractive to incumbents if the cost and complexity of entry are high. So, for example, industries with a large laid-down investment, such as major manufacturing or mining, are thought to be high. An industry is considered to be unattractive, and therefore to be avoided by new entrants, if it is subject to high regulation or exposure to political or reputational risk. New disruptors will turn their attention to less-problematical sectors.

These traditional wisdoms are now being challenged.

Take the example of the replacement of the internal combustion engine by alternative means of propulsion, particularly the *electric car*. Until a couple years ago, most people would have thought the massive laid-down investment in the automobile industry would have made car makers immune to such fundamental disruption. Not so now. Many observers are predicting the tipping point for the electric car with the launch of the Tesla Model S, a beautiful vehicle supplied with free recharging from a distribution network including solar-powered recharging stations. Investors are now taking electric cars and electric recharging distribution networks seriously, sowing fear into the hearts of Detroit, Big Car and the oil industry. Major auto manufacturers are accelerating the roll out of their own electric car offerings. And the driverless car is no longer a dream, with giants like Google now major players.

You might think that the massive cost of launch of satellites and delivery of payloads to the International Space Station (ISS) would mean that *aerospace* would remain the preserve of governments in the pursuit of long-term strategic ambitions. And so it was for many decades. In the US, NASA was commissioning launches from Boeing and Lockheed using legacy rocket technology and avionics supplied by the Russians. Progressively, Ariane (the European Space Agency), the Russians directly, the Chinese and now India undercut the traditional delivery systems and took increasing market share, particularly for the launch of satellites. Private US space companies such as Orbital Sciences Corporation, Bigelow and SpaceX saw the disruption opportunity to take on the seemingly complacent big boys by developing new rocket technologies and delivery systems that would transform the business model and value networks of the established players. SpaceX, in particular, has made the whole industry sit up and rethink itself, especially with the successful recovery of a Falcon 9 rocket landing on a barge in the Atlantic, opening up the prospect of reusing rockets and the revolutionizing of the economics of the industry.

If such industries are showing signs on disruption, why is that *banking* seems to have been relatively immune so far? Surely the antiquated practices and the widespread presence of value-eroding intermediaries between principals and customers make mainstream banks ripe for disruption. After all, other industries great and small such as media and retailing, hotels and taxis, and now automobiles, aerospace and (solar) energy, are being revolutionized by digital giants and start-ups alike, with incumbents seeming to be in terminal decline. Admittedly, crowdfunding, peer-to-peer lending, fintech startups, roboadvisors and challenger banks are all manifestations of disruption at the margins – but where is the fundamental disruption? Perhaps not so far away!

Digital giants like Google are on the record as being put off by the regulatory barriers to entry and the reputational risk from involvement in banking – just think of the low esteem of bank brands since the financial crisis in 2007! There are other fish to fry! A company like Google would, in theory, be attracted to apply its expertise to disrupt the payments and international settlements that underpin the financial services industry. The opaque, multi-layered and high commission-based costs of intermediaries make the payments and settlement system ripe for digital disruption. And the principal intermediaries, the traditional incumbent banks, would be dangerously threatened.

They are put off by the major barrier to entry of the iron grip, which the oligopolistic banking incumbents exercise over the payments system through the central banks. Fundamental disruption is only likely to happen if and when the central banks see a way that they themselves can control a transition to a more efficient payments and settlement order. After all, the international payments system and infrastructure impact virtually every part of the financial services industry, and the central banks put their integrity above anything else – they are guarantors of settlement, and they will brook no risk to its integrity.

Nevertheless, things are changing. There are signs that this fundamental disruption to traditional banking intermediation may be on the way. There is already an alternative, low-cost currency and payment system out there in the form of Bitcoin. Underpinned by the blockchain digital technology, Bitcoin has already more than proved itself, much to the traditional players' chagrin. A recent report from Santander estimated that Bitcoin could save lenders up to $20 billion a year in settlement, regulation and cross-border payment costs.

The importance of the blockchain has been somewhat masked by the bad press for Bitcoin, seen by many to be the preserve of money launderers and those seeking to avoid regulatory oversight. In fact, the blockchain infrastructure behind Bitcoin is a ready-made alternative open platform for payments, which has worked brilliantly. The blockchain technology is itself pretty uncontroversial: an open record of digital events, distributed among many different parties, which can only be updated by consensus of a majority of the participants in the system, and where information can never be erased. The blockchain contains a verifiable record of every single transaction ever made on the Bitcoin (or other) transaction platform it sustains. And the blockchain is tamper-resistant and each block in the chain is enforced cryptographically – so the security of the platform is reassuring to demanding potential users such as central banks.

Central banks are reappraising the future of their settlement systems and a blockchain-based alternative must be on their radar screens. Stock markets are also seeing if they can gain competitive advantage from new platforms. Indeed, the Australian Stock Exchange recently announced that it is developing a blockchain as a replacement for its platform for the clearing and settlement of trades. London and other exchanges are considering the same.

So, as these examples show, all top management teams need to accept the reality of fundamental disruption in their industry, whatever it is.

TRIGGERS OF ACCEPTANCE

Things that trigger acceptance may occur naturally, but they can also be created (*see Figure 11*).

Triggers of Acceptance

- Crisis
- (New) Leadership
- Reading
- Seeing
- Health Check

FIGURE 11 – TRIGGERS OF ACCEPTANCE CAN OCCUR NATURALLY OR BE CREATED.

CRISIS

A crisis may be an event or a circumstance, which is clear to all (for example, insolvency or loss of a major piece of business). On the other hand, a state of denial by senior executives can lead to a progressive decline in self-esteem, expressed by anger, confusion and depression, ultimately leading to a sense of crisis. The organization itself gets to feel it, despite the best efforts of management. If not crisis, then a widespread sense of malaise about the place can be a precondition for acceptance. What a colleague described as "an atmosphere of doom." Share price, profit announcements, market analysts' reports, scandals and competitors' success can all aggravate symptoms of malaise. It is a truism that companies that are doing well within their traditional business model and value networks rarely see the need to transform. They need a sense of a "burning platform" – an obligation to change. Unfortunately, a crisis can come when disruption is well advanced and the scope for transformational change is then limited.

Thankfully, there are many examples of companies that have seen a crisis coming and have reacted to it – Intel, Dell, Adidas and Lego come to mind.

(NEW) LEADERSHIP

As with most transformations, the most obvious trigger is leadership, usually new leadership, either on the board or at the CEO level. Here is a powerful example.

My colleagues and I have been warning top executives in the hotel industry for more than 10 years that they are asleep at the switch, ignoring the disruptions that will affect their industry. There was an opportunity to create a real market between suppliers of hotel beds, to personalize the hotel stay to the traveller by adding concierge experiences in the hotel and the locality, and to distribute directly to consumers and interest groups, bypassing expensive and value-eroding intermediaries.

Instead they allowed disruptive intermediaries, the Online Travel Agencies (OTAs) such as Expedia and specialist reservation sites such as Booking, to dominate the distribution space. And they virtually ignored meta-search and the arrival of room-share offerings such as Airbnb.

Despairing of the complacency of the large chains, who concentrated on their own websites and merely added multichannel features to their offerings, my colleagues and I spent much energy trying to convince the multitude of small independent hotels and in-destination providers of experiences to come together to achieve a real market with the features that the digital world enables, with the potential to bypass, at least partially, the value-eroding intermediaries. But to no avail. Hotels, both large and small, continued to do their own thing.

But then suddenly one of the largest hotel chains woke up – it has accepted denial and is determined to "get cracking." Sebastien Bazin was appointed chairman and CEO of Accor Hotels in 2013. He has recognized the reality of the Christiansen doctrine that established enterprises allowed the disruptors to disrupt, but seems determined to fight back.

Interviewed in November 2015 by the industry website Skift (Schaal, 2015), Bazin said: "Accor is not going to be a spectator of its own life. We're an actor." He went on to say, "All of us. For the last 15 years, we've been sleeping. I said that publicly and I got yelled at by my peers. Let's face it, we've missed three waves in the digital revolution. The first wave was 12 years ago, the OTAs. Did we move? No, of course not. Yeah, we tried Roomkey. *Pschitt.* (The French slang term doesn't have a direct translation, but it comes from the sound of opening a can of soda, as in something that blew up.) We missed it. We felt, I guess, it (the OTAs) would be inconsequential. Yeah, well it's now a big feature, and we should have actually paid attention. Then, three or four years later it was metasearch. Did we do anything about it? Of course not. We've done nothing. Then the OTAs vertically integrated, buying Kayak and buying Trivago so they actually figured it out. Number three is the sharing economy. Have we missed it? Did we move with Airbnb, and Uber, and Lending Club? Yeah, we're certainly watching and we're saying, 'Well, we better move.' Well, it's about time to move because we're going to have a fourth wave and a fifth wave." Wow. Good luck, Sebastien!

How is it that Accor was able to wake up so fundamentally, while the industry and his predecessors seemed asleep at the switch? Significantly, Sebastien is an outsider. This seems to have been the precondition for Accor to break out of the inbreeding syndrome constraint described in chapter 7. Significantly, he had a private equity background and served as CEO, principal and managing director of Europe at Colony Capital, one of the largest private equity real estate funds in the world, based in San Francisco, with significant investments in hotel assets, including Accor. He came in with a productive disruptor's mindset, looking at Accor's business model and value networks with a fresh pair of eyes.

READING

Top executives read a lot of business books – airport bookstalls thrive on this reality. Just look at the yards of shelf space devoted to leadership in Barnes & Noble or on Amazon. In fact, if senior executives are like me, they "skim read" a lot, trying to extract the essence of the message from the voluminous pages of text. At the back of this book, you will find a selection of books, articles and links that are worth more than a "skim read," which could make you feel comfortable in accepting the reality of the disruption around the corner, and provide clues on how to deal with it. I have referred to most of them in this book. You are neither alone, nor an oddball, in agonizing about the scope, reach, pace and need for disruptive change! Reading can certainly help in attaining a sense of calm acceptance.

SEEING

There is nothing quite like the experience of total immersion in the realities of the disruptive world to help the move from acceptance in principle to acceptance in reality. I was pleased to arrange, through colleagues at Elixirr, a "deep dive" visit by the top team of a large consumer insurance and financial services group to Silicon Valley. Back-to-back meetings with potentially disruptive innovators and venture capitalists, interspersed with consumer testing, real-time solution design workshops, and challenges to their old world view from leaders of start-ups, combined to generate a feeling that disruptive change was a reality and that they could be part of it. The CEO reported on "The level of excitement in each of us to change. I'm keen to get back to steer and join… and get cracking. But I am under no illusion that we'll reflect on the trip as the 'easy bit' and I feel it has given us such clear focus and that we'll succeed in our ambition."

This opening of the eyes, coupled with the sense that the moment of clarity or revelation is the "easy bit" – and that we must now "get cracking" – are clear signals of the acceptance that we are talking about here.

TAKING A "HEALTH CHECK"

It can help to get an objective assessment of how fit your business is to survive disruption against major variables. One such simple diagnostic tool can be found on the Elixirr website (https://toolkit.elixirr.com/), and no doubt others exist.

Vulnerability – how vulnerable is your industry? Clearly, information-intensive, consumer-service industries are highly vulnerable to disruptive business models and new value networks. Many have already been disrupted (think photography, music, research) and others are ripe for it. It was only a couple of years ago that I was pointing out the emerging disruptive threat of what are now well-established "roboadvisers" (such as Nutmeg) to the CEO of a major financial advice and wealth management corporation. After all, Big Data and deep learning algorithmic analysis of volunteered and derived customer data on lifestyle and appetite for risk lend themselves perfectly to the online world. And regulators prefer bypassing human advice.

As we saw earlier in this chapter, even capital-intensive industries, such as oil and gas, mining, aerospace, construction, manufacturing and transportation can be disrupted, even though at first sight they are less vulnerable to disruption from new innovators. While possibly true for drilling holes, for example, this is not true for the whole plethora of oil field production and distribution services, which are well advanced along the disruptive business model path. And in the factory, robotics and the "internet of things" can transform the economics of established players, as well as present opportunities for disruptive new players. And remember the disruptive effect that machine learning has on pretty much all the functions of the enterprise within the platform-thinking world!

Readiness – how aware is your business and how is it structured in the face of disruption? For example, is disruptive change (as opposed to incremental change) on the agenda? Are there informal structures within which disruptive innovations can breed without being stifled? What about the board and top management – is there a serious conversation going on about disruption?

Assets – how strong are your capabilities and resources to handle disruptive change? For example, do you think your brands, your investment assets, technology platform, and supplier relationships, "protect you" from disruptive forces? Where are the sustainable barriers to entry, if any?

A combined health check reading from the whole top team can be a useful basis for a serious conversation about acceptance and a desire to "get cracking."

SEEDING THE NEW REALITY

I like the story recounted by Christian Madsbjerg and Mikkel Rasmussen in their book, *The Moment of Clarity* (Madsbjerg, 2014), about Genevieve Bell, who greatly influenced Intel in rethinking what it was about. Her recruitment started with a chance encounter in a bar and a discussion on anthropology. Before long, she was had joined Intel and was leading a group rebranded "People and Practices Research Lab," which was, as its name implies, a radical shift within the engineering culture that so dominated Intel. "Moore's Law stated that semiconductors were going to get smaller, but it didn't tell us anything about what people were going to do with them or why a consumer would be interested. It started to become increasingly clear to all of us that consumers just didn't care about the same things we cared about." Bell acted as a persistent irritant within the business, supported by leaders who knew that what she was researching was important for the survival of the firm. She was an official "productive disruptor", as I described in chapter 7 - a "maverick with a licence to annoy," as a CEO friend of mine put it in another context. At his last meeting as CEO at Intel, Craig Barrett introduced Bell to the three hundred most important decision makers and managers in the company. Bell, an Australian, recalls: "Craig gets up before I speak, and he tells the room, 'I want you to listen to this woman. She may have a funny accent, and she may not be like the rest of us, but she is the future of the company, so pay attention.'"

It is not so much the "what" of disruption, but more the "so what?" for dealing with the new reality that needs to be "seeded." For example:
- We must assume that our current business model, and the upstream and downstream value networks that support it, will be replaced by different, lower-cost, and more responsive models for the Digital Age. We will never be able to compete head-to-head with new innovators.
- We must think fundamentally differently about our business as part of an ecosystem meeting the needs of our customers.
- We must move from a "pipe" model to a "platform" model for our business, and prioritize investment in this.

- We must create the environment for innovation to thrive and for new businesses to grow, which are not stifled by our orthodox organizational processes.
- We need to initiate the reinvention of how we perform functional support services, rather than be dragged kicking and screaming when they happen.

CHAPTER 10

DEVELOPING A PLATFORM-COMPATIBLE BUSINESS MODEL

Everyone is building platforms! Over many years, my sister and her husband have been preparing Christian aid workers in practical on-the-ground skills, including cross-cultural training for working in completely different environments. Their methods have proved their worth and are in high demand. They need to scale! There is no need to recruit and ramp up their physical organization – they are developing their own Massive Open Online Course (MOOC) learning experience, in which participants pass through a testing, evaluation and accreditation process, coached by online tutors. Potentially, they could rapidly have hundreds of workers with the right skills ready to go.

But platforms need to be right for you. Once you have reached a state of acceptance, and acquired a determination to "get cracking," you also will need to evolve your business model to enable you to compete in the rapidly evolving digitally disruptive world that we characterized in the first part of this book. You will need to develop your own platform-compatible business model. I call this "platform compatible" because this is what it will be – evolving to a platform model and introducing platform-compatible features from the get-go.

I find that many top executives are quite anxious about this. They understand the realities of how their legacy IT structure, systems and processes are out of kilter with the nimble platform business models of "digital native" companies, both large and small. They fear the cost, complexity and timeframe required to transform to compete. But all is not lost. You can migrate to a platform model in stages, taking the best of your legacy, opening it up to external platforms, and innovating with digitally enabled and platform-enabled capability. Read on!

THE IMPERATIVE FOR PLATFORM FEATURES IN YOUR NEW BUSINESS MODEL

First of all, let us be clear why taking determined steps to creating a platform-compatible business model is, like acceptance, a precondition for an established enterprise in a traditional industry to survive in the disruptive world. There are three main reasons:

1. **Licence to operate** – unless you have platform features, you will be unable to operate in the disruptive world. We discovered earlier that the combination of the cloud (and the data analytical capability it enables), mobile and social media – disruptive technological forces – transforms the way new generations think about life and how they behave as they live it. These forces are the air that "digital natives"

breathe, and to mix my metaphor, the sea in which they swim. When it comes to consuming the products and services of your enterprise, they go about informing themselves, deciding and judging in completely different ways than in the past. As we saw in chapter 3, their needs and what they buy are strongly influenced by the community in which they live – their friends and family. This community is made up of actual friends and family encountered in the physical world, but also online friends they may never actually meet. They and the people they encounter on social media with whom they have an affinity react badly to having things pushed out and sold to them down "pipes." Actually, they do not really understand this approach. In short, they and you live in an ecosystem within which you and they swim and interact, alongside all the other providers that may be of interest in the lives of potential consumers within it. Your challenge is to be an active participant in this ecosystem, to open yourself to it, so that you participate in the exchange of conversations, experiences, recommendations and feedback that take place within the ecosystem – and earn a licence to operate in this new ecosystem world.

2. **Scalability** – as my sister is discovering, a platform-enabled business model will enable you to scale your business beyond your wildest dreams. With proper design, you will no longer be constrained by incremental steps of new investment in capacity and capability. Your model will have the built-in capability to meet the needs of your customers and business partners as required and in probably unpredictable ways. But beware, therein also lies the danger – rapid scale without properly thinking about how to service the demand can lead to catastrophe. The offer must be able to meet the volume demanded.

3. **Market value** – as Pankaj Ghemawat, the well-known author and speaker, has recently pointed out, markets are looking deeper at the intangible value lurking within your company in assessment of enterprise value. And one of the most important elements of intangible value will be the business model that sustains your business, and whether or not it has the platform features that will enable you to participate seamlessly on pure-play platforms, on external commercial platforms, or by creating a proprietary platform for your own needs. A study attributed to Ghemawat showed that in 1986, 58% of the market value of an enterprise was derived from tangible assets, but this proportion had fallen to 24% in 2013. Put another way, being seen to have the right

enabling intangible asset of a business model with appropriate platform features should translate directly into share price and stock market value.

In chapter 4, we saw that an unreconstructed, legacy "pipes" business model will not be fit for purpose in the disruptive age. This is a business model where value is produced upstream and is pushed to consumers downstream, creating a linear flow of value, much like water flowing through a pipe. It had evolved to meet the needs of the previous industrial ages. We explored the alternative platform business model as expounded by Sangeet Choudary, and we characterized what a revolution a pure-play platform business model would imply. The primary currency on the platform would be data.

We saw that you would need to evolve your business model from this "pipes" view toward a "platform" view (*see Figure 12*). In the construction industry, the general contractor builds a platform on which a multiplicity of trades can work and interact in pursuit of the common aim of completing the building. You would need to do the same.

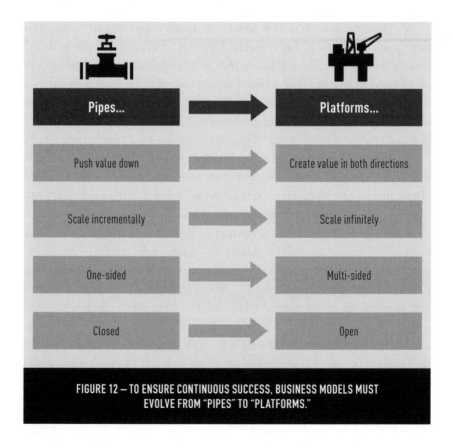

FIGURE 12 – TO ENSURE CONTINUOUS SUCCESS, BUSINESS MODELS MUST EVOLVE FROM "PIPES" TO "PLATFORMS."

The nature of your platform would depend on the industry you are in. If you are in a resources extraction or manufacturing industry, for example, your platform would tend to be focused on "the internet of things" – opening yourself up into the ecosystem of engineers, researchers, universities, product designers and other entities on which automation and other enhancements to the means of extraction or the features of your manufactured product depend. If your industry is information-intensive, your platform would be constructed for intelligent exchange of data for the mutual benefit of your customers and their and your partners.

But a word of caution. There has been a lot of hype about platform business models in recent years. You might get the impression that the only way forward for all businesses is to discard the legacy "pipe" and go all-out for a platform model straight away, in one bound. This can be dangerous, and, as we will see below, unnecessary. But you will certainly need to adopt some of the attributes as you adapt with a business model that is right for you and open yourself up so that you participate on others' platforms.

Think of the laws of nature when you decide where you fit in the platform world – after all, this is surely the purest ecosystem of all! As in the natural world, there are predators and prey at all links in the food chain, all adapted to the needs of where they sit and what they need to survive. The lion has evolved a different "platform" of equipment for its needs than those needed by the green finch or the ant. Obvious? Perhaps, but similarly, you need to think of the kind of platform you need for your ecosystem.

In chapter 4, we explored four different types of platforms – pure-play platforms (Google, Apple, social media), commercial platforms (Amazon, eBay), proprietary platforms (owned and operated by an incumbent business) and cooperative platforms (marketplaces for multiple suppliers).

A pure-play platform enables others to interact and transact, earning a kind of toll fee for use of the platform – think social media or YouTube. On a commercial platform, the owner acts as a principal, selling his own brands and products and listing at a sharp negotiated price others' brands and products just like a multiple retailer – like Amazon. A cooperative platform creates a market for multiple owners to provide value to customers and their ecosystems directly. You will need to develop a business model that opens you up to interactions on all these kinds of platforms, as well as enabling customers, suppliers and their respective ecosystems to interact directly on your own proprietary platform. This is the challenge of developing your platform-compatible business model.

THE CHALLENGE TO DEVELOPING YOUR OWN PLATFORM

Sangeet Choudary explains that moving toward a platform model implies doing things in the reverse order than you are used to. For a start-up, the journey to platform scale starts with the infrastructure layer of the platform – the network or ecosystem layer comes next and the data layer last. In contrast, "The journey to platform scale for a large pipe-based business starts with the data layer." This certainly chimes with my experience and that of my colleagues as we accompany large, established pipe-based businesses on the journey toward becoming a platform. Modelling the data you have is where you start – often a revealing process in itself.

Choudary (Choudary, 2015) describes the necessary steps, and challenges, on the journey toward becoming a platform business, summarized here:

1. *Build a culture of data acquisition.* The primary purpose of all innovations, including apps and websites, becomes the acquisition of data. Seeding the new culture of data acquisition becomes the primary focus of the platform-creator.

2. *Enable data porosity and integration.* "The pipe business must integrate all processes, workflows and touchpoints at the data layer. Pipe businesses must restructure their internal systems to be more data-porous. This requires the implementation of internal APIs. Today, most organizations leverage IT as a backend infrastructure, but their business units work in silos and do not communicate with each other. There is minimal data exchange between business units. To eventually leverage platform scale, pipe organizations must be data-porous. Most importantly, they must have a unified view of the user. Every user should be represented by a unique data entry."

3. *Leverage implicit data-driven network effects.* You build on the unique advantage you have as a large pipe-based business when compared to a start up – access to a large user base. Once a user has a unique reference in the data layer, you can now start to leverage the network effect to the users you already have – "Did you know that a user like you also bought this?" Like Amazon.

4. *Build explicit communities.* Once the first steps have been executed, you can start promoting explicit communities within your database – for example, a cruise line can identify the network of transactions that a loyal cruiser has done on board and encourage the

creation of an industry community around the cruise line's itineraries and experiences.

5. *Enable explicit exchange.* At this final stage, the full exchange has been created, with data being the commodity exchanged for mutual value. Users are now connected and are being led to new interactions. The ecosystem of products and services around the user, of which you are a part, is fully active. The full benefits of the platform model become apparent.

For established enterprises in traditional industries, there is both bad news and good news in meeting the challenge.

First the bad news. If you are a large, established business, your organization is designed to the needs of a "pipes" business – optimizing established systems and processes. It does not have the agility to respond to what is needed in building a "platform." Cumbersome "waterfall" approaches to large system changes are still prevalent and unresponsive to the rapidly changing digital scene. IT people are stuck in their ways. Platform innovation requires different performance measurement metrics – it may take several years for the full benefits to take off. Obliging platform innovators to meet the short-term benefit delivery timescales described earlier in this book will be distracting and even counterproductive. There may not be obvious "low-hanging fruit" to be plucked. You do not have a view of the world that focuses on consumers and external interaction. Data is seen as a proprietary corporate asset to be protected, not the primary currency of the business and as a resource to be expanded and shared. In short, your biggest disadvantage is that you do not have a culture of data acquisition, management and sharing, nor an understanding of the ecosystem.

But there is good news. You have been around for a long time and you will have built large pipes that serve maybe millions of users. You have established unique user access through the power of your brands and relationships in your existing value networks. You have massive amounts of data (even though most may lie fallow and unproductive). And if you have reached a state of acceptance and understand at the highest level the strategic existential imperative for action, then you may have more capital and experienced resources to deploy than a start-up could ever dream of.

You need to look at your "pipes" legacy in a new way. Given the tools and techniques that are now available, it is not a question of taking a wrecking ball to the legacy and embarking upon a programme of creating a whole new platform from scratch. That would take forever, cost a fortune, and be wasteful and unnecessary. Nor is it a question of installing a layer of middleware with APIs on top of your old legacy systems and expecting that this will meet your needs and solve your problems. At best, this will only produce an improved "pipes" model. And much middleware has itself become "legacy," so you will be layering legacy on top of legacy.

You have jewels, some known, others yet to be discovered, lurking within your legacy. And you are better at mining for them and using them than you think! So how do you exploit the existing within the legacy and at the same time innovate, opening up your system and processes to the ecosystem we have been describing?

IMPLEMENTING YOUR PLATFORM-COMPATIBLE BUSINESS MODEL

You will need to see the move to a platform as the "higher purpose" for your business model. But this will be a journey.

The technology research company, Gartner, has expounded the notion of a bimodal capability to change in the Digital Age – a marriage of a linear approach, emphasizing predictability and stability, with a nonlinear approach (Gartner, 2015). This helpful thinking has gained widespread traction in business circles and is a useful framework approach for getting the best from the "pipes legacy," while also introducing the "platform-like" innovation you will require. In effect, you need to be in both innovation mode and the legacy mode at the same time. And your execution plan must accommodate both.

Innovating at the front end without accommodating the legacy at the back end can be frustrating, is all too common from my experience – and can seriously derail well-intentioned digital innovation initiatives.

Initially, you should seek to optimize your "pipes" legacy by mining data more effectively and applying algorithms that allow you to be more effective in meeting customer needs, and to eliminate waste of the products and services you produce. Such an optimization approach will require you to adopt a data-driven mindset and obsession, as described by Choudary (Choudary, 2015). Many businesses will already be doing this – the purview of so many digital transformation programmes I come across. While important, you should nevertheless only see this as an interim step to the right platform-compatible business model hybrid or pure play, whichever will be right for you.

You will want to identify and structure the data that lies within the unstructured data deep in your legacy systems. One of the challenges in dealing with legacy is that often the people trying to untangle it did not build it, and there are few records of how it works – so operating around the black box is a delicate piece of work – and these days, an unnecessary approach. There are tools and capabilities – burrowing worms or robots – to get behind the green screen of the mainframe, through the business logic to the data layer and pluck out the data that are relevant to your need – and open it out to the external ecosystem. Basically we are talking about "hacking" into the legacy to extract the bits we need.

A TWO-STEP APPROACH

David Mullins and his team at Elixirr have shown that slavishly following widespread current thinking and attempting to create a platform in one bound can be a dangerous mistake.

As the Venn diagram overleaf illustrates, attempting to move from existing legacy (bottom left) to platform (top) as one process is "playing too hard," and such a radical transformation may be doomed to failure (*see Figure 13*). We have certainly seen this reality within a large international service business. What proved to be an overly ambitious attempt to create a digital platform confronted problems of understanding, readiness, leadership, technology and absence of talent that forced it to grind to a halt. The unintended disruptive consequences of moving to a digital platform was, indeed, playing too hard and the organization rejected it. It moved back across the feedback ellipse to the current state, and time, energy, money and momentum were all lost.

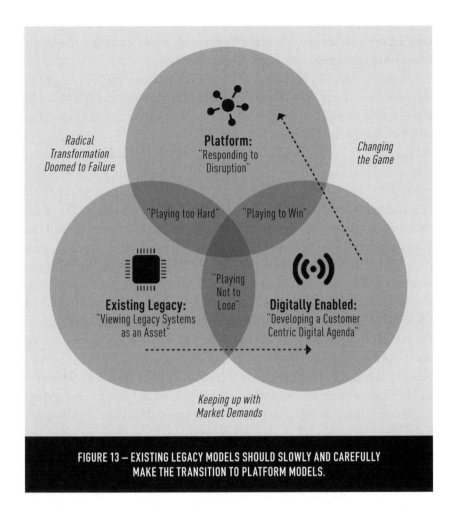

FIGURE 13 – EXISTING LEGACY MODELS SHOULD SLOWLY AND CAREFULLY
MAKE THE TRANSITION TO PLATFORM MODELS.

The sensible approach is in two steps. The first is to consider legacy systems as assets to be exploited and recast (not things to be junked) and to move to the bottom right of the diagram, "playing not to lose" by becoming digitally enabled – developing a customer-centric digital agenda, which all can understand and relate to. This means mining into the data within the legacy in the ways described by Choudary and integrating digitally with the innovations at the front end – putting in place APIs as a precursor to moving to a platform. Indeed such digital enablement through the APIs should already let you participate in external platforms. This stepped approach allows an established enterprise within a traditional industry, which has the imperative to innovate with its customers at the front end, to "stay in the game" and take actions that are not too ambitious, which would endanger the whole transformation agenda and will be doomed to failure.

As you execute the first stage of digital enablement, you will be laying the groundwork for your platform-compatible business model. You will then be able to plan for, and digest, the journey to the full platform. You will then be able to "play to win."

But how to go about this first stage to becoming a digitally enabled business? How many times have you heard of situations where management teams get fired up with innovations to their businesses at the front end and then hit a brick wall when they get back to the ranch? The innovations they have planned to systems of engagement meet the inertia of the back end, the systems of record. Some of my partners recently spent a week with a CEO and his top team in Silicon Valley, introducing them to the venture capital community and a range of start-ups having the potential to disrupt their business model or to help them innovate. They returned fired up with innovation possibilities at the front end of the business. Back at the ranch, they came across a classic obstacle. The things they wanted to do at the front end – to their "systems of engagement" – were impossible, said IT. The back office "systems of record" could not cope with what was needed. But perhaps we could do some "work around," people were saying.

The important thing to recognize is that you will fail – or certainly get frustrated and blown off track – if you try to make the systems of record conform after the event to what you want to innovate with at the front end. You must work in parallel, not in sequence; in harness, not in conflict. And you must be realistic, evolving your digital enablement of your offerings in light of the obstacles and realities. You must embrace the paradox, recognize the mutually dependent opposites – you must inhale and exhale at the same time! In short, you must become a leader for the disruptive age (*see chapter 14*).

While you are discovering, creating, testing and choosing your innovations, you are at the same time analysing the realities within the systems of record, identifying the roadblocks, the rocks to be navigated round, the ways to deal with them and the response possibilities. So when you have your Minimal Viable Products (MVPs) ready to go, the plans for dealing with the legacy in the sytems of record are also ready to go, and you are already in the process of implementation!

Face it, you will come across fundamental rocks in the way. Remember that these rocks are not necessarily technology obstacles – in fact, from my experience, the rocks are more usually human! For example, attitudes may need shifting – what is in fact possible, and what can be done to break the rocks into smaller rocks to make them more easily dealt with. You may have "energy sappers" who are neutering effectiveness (see Chapter 14). And you may lack the skill sets.

Once you have aligned the implementation plans for the MVPs of your systems of engagement with your migration and rollout steps within the systems of record, you will be ready for a sustainable first stage on the journey to having a platform-compatible business model. New solution providers, such as Ravn or OpenLegacy, are out there to help you structure and implement. Here is a pitch from OpenLegacy's website, which certainly sounds good!

"OpenLegacy is the world's first and only lightweight, nonintrusive solution for automated legacy modernization and enterprise application integration. With its API-based, open-standards platform, OpenLegacy enables enterprises to rapidly extend on-premise systems to mobile, web and cloud applications, delivering risk-free, high-impact results that solve immediate business needs.

OpenLegacy's standard tools rapidly extract the services and information from within legacy systems into an editable format that puts the power of integration into the enterprises' hands, without the expensive handcuffs of vendor lock-in. Once a business process is exposed – which can be done in minutes – the output can automatically be transformed into stand-alone mobile, web, and cloud applications, and connected with other solutions. Most importantly, no changes are required to the on-premise system in order for OpenLegacy to work – the process is risk-free.

Building on open-standard protocols, OpenLegacy's approach harnesses API technology to enable enterprises to quickly, easily and freely extend their back-end services to the cutting-edge while maintaining the enterprise's robust and reliable legacy systems – without vendor lock-in. Moreover, OpenLegacy can seamlessly work within the framework of current Services Oriented Architecture (SOA)." (OpenLegacy, 2016)

Once you have completed Stage 1 – moving to a customer-centric digital agenda – you will be ready and able to move to your full platform-compatible business model, "playing to win." Your platform will enable the interaction between supply and demand, between your customers and their ecosystem, and your products and services and your ecosystem of suppliers and relationships. You will probably have a "platform of platforms," your own proprietary platform, complemented by presence on external pure play and commercial platforms. Your platform-compatible business model will be specific to you!

TESTING FOR SUCCESS

How will you know that you have made it to your platform-compatible business model?

Should you aspire to be like YouTube, which owns nothing beyond the platform itself, you could own few assets beyond the platform, a few highly talented people, and the valuable interactions that take place across the platform. Remember Lao Tzu's wisdom (*see chapter 4*)! So the migration to such a pure-play platform implies a radical review of the nature of partnerships and relationships, and the creation of what Clayton Christiansen calls new value networks based upon interactions across your platform.

You should be open to a fundamental recasting of your business if the opportunity exists for such a pure-play platform. In the pure-play end state, manufacturing and distribution of your brands may become perceived as a "service" to the customers using your platform, in much the same way Amazon customers see the superlative delivery service provided as a bolt-on service to what they buy in the online store. Little do most people know of the state-of-the-art warehousing, logistics and third-party delivery infrastructure and system optimization service that lie behind the scenes. The same may apply to other activities and functions that you provide in-house. Conceptually, you outsource everything but the needs of the interactions across the platform.

Not many businesses' business models will go this far, at least not in the early stages of the journey. As you complete the execution of your projects, you will see platform effects take root as you (and they) see the value created to customers from interactions with you and other organizations within their ecosystem. New value-creating relationships and partnerships get created with sometimes surprising bedfellows outside your traditional orbit.

Short of the pure-play platform model, how will you know that you have adopted the right platform characteristics for your business model? The real test of success will be when you have effortless data exchange and mutually beneficial interactions with your customers and partners and with the other members of their ecosystem. You will know this when products and services are developed in real time to meet individual consumer's needs, when inventory is drastically reduced, when production planning is seamless... and so on.

Whatever else you will have done, you will have opened up your data layers to your consumers, their social networks, and the external platforms on which they may be active. To do this, you will have been through all the stages: mine, reveal, structure, digitize, curate and render useful. You will know you have been successful when your customers see you and your data differently.

Let me explain this in an example. My wife and I recently had a short stay in Barcelona. It is a wonderful destination. You can find out about it through multiple media – Barcelona.com, Lonely Planet, Trip Advisor, guidebooks of all kinds and reservation sites for airlines and hotels such as Booking or Expedia. What all these sites do is make you aware of "stuff" – they only give you a flavour of what the Barcelona experience really is. You would know a real Barcelona platform if it was a one-stop shop for you to absorb and share experiences, likes and dislikes, with people like you. The "stuff" of available opportunities would become secondary to the feelings you would gain from the potential visit you would make. The online Barcelona platform's emphasis would shift:

- From utilization to utility
- From consumption to passion
- From price to worth
- From flat to 3D
- From features to values
- From push to open access
- From proprietary to universal
- From mine to ours.

When your customers see you in this kind of way, when they interact on your and others' platforms, you will know that you are getting there.

As you start to recast your business in line with your platform-compatible business model, commercial success will become obvious. For example, you will start to generate exponential user growth due to network effects derived from the interactions across your own and external platforms. You will be able to take great chunks of cost previously dedicated to a "pipes" model out of your operations.

You will know when you are there by the change of atmosphere within your company. The journey will transform your organization – the people, the way you work and the processes you apply. If all goes well, the "viscosity index" will improve – things will be lighter, easier to achieve and faster. You will be nimbler. This will be the best test of success of all!

CONCLUSIONS

Embarking upon the journey toward your platform-compatible business model will be vital to survival, let alone success, in the disruptive world.

The nature of the right platform-compatible business model for you will be different depending on your industry. A platform of the "internet of things" will tend to be appropriate for resources, heavy manufacturing and capital-intensive industries. A data exchange platform will tend to be a required element for information-intensive industries.

All platform-compatible business models will need to open up your organization's systems and processes to your customers and business partners. Your model will offer a data exchange in which customers interact with you and other providers of products and services within the personal ecosystems of your customers. Customers will be able to find your products or services as well as others' products and services on your and others' platforms, either directly or through invisible links – think Amazon again! The platform promotes interactions – you "listen" and react to your customers as much as they react (and hopefully purchase!) through you.

As you advance in your journey to your platform-compatible business model, you will be able to rethink your value networks and the structure of your business activities – perhaps "outsourcing" manufacturing, distribution and other traditional activities and functions.

Your business model will need to open you up to interactions and transactions on external platforms, as well as enabling customers, suppliers and their respective ecosystems to interact directly on your own proprietary platform. You will need to have APIs linking you to pure-play platforms, which enable others to interact and transact, earning a kind of toll fee for use of the platform – like YouTube; and to commercial platforms, where the owner acts as a principal, selling his own brands and products and listing at a sharp negotiated price others' brands and products just like a multiple retailer – like Amazon.

You should see your "legacy" as an asset, not a liability. But you need a "bimodal" mindset, embracing the old and the new in parallel while retaining the long-term higher purpose of a "business as interactions."

The sensible implemenation approach is in two steps. You start by becoming digitally enabled, mining the data and integrating digitally with the innovations at the front end – putting in place APIs as a precursor to moving to a platform. This allows you to play in the platform space by participating in external platforms and to "stay in the game," to take actions that are not too ambitious, won't endanger the whole transformation agenda, and won't be doomed to failure.

You need to execute innovations at the front end (systems of engagement) in parallel with changes to your back end (systems of record). The integrated process described above will allow you to execute the minimal viable products you want to introduce effectively.

Your implementation programme can use new tools and techniques (including burrowing worms and robots), now widely available, to extract the data you need from the legacy within the innovative platform framework you establish and to execute the APIs required for you to open up your business model.

Moving to a full platform business model (playing to win) will follow seamlessly upon the foundations created in the first stage – many of the rocks and roadblocks to progress will have been identified and dealt with. The full nature of the right platform-compatible business model will also have become clear.

It will be a challenge, but vital nevertheless, to get all stakeholders (owners, board, executive team, key influencers and business partners) to understand the evolution toward the innovative platform-compatible business model containing the platform features described. They need to fully understand and act upon what it involves in terms of funding commitments and persistence. The right leadership and talent will be critical for success.

CHAPTER 11

MAKING A BIG MOVE — "DOING A DELL"

So far, I have suggested that there are two fundamental steps needed, whatever else an established enterprise does, to move beyond denial and to survive in a disrupted world:

- Reach a state of acceptance with a resolve to "get cracking"
- Build your platform-compatible business model with "platform" features.

I suggest that these are the *sine qua non* requirements for the long-term survival of your company. After all, if you cannot recognize reality and the need to do something serious about it, there is no point in moving further. And unless you change your business model away from a "pipes" view to a "platform-enabled ecosystem" view, then there is little hope.

Thereafter, there are theoretical choices to be made. I say theoretical since, in the first case, making a big move – "Doing a Dell"– doesn't mean that every enterprise will have the vision and wherewithal to so thoroughly transform itself by moving from a strong position in a maturing and aging market to a new, but related, growing market offering long-term attractive prospects.

This is what Dell has done. Even though Dell is an interesting, but possibly exceptional case, the story can help as a framework for established quoted enterprises in considering their futures.

THE HIGHS AND LOWS OF A DISRUPTIVE INNOVATOR

Dell was a serial disruptor, was then disrupted and seemed powerless to respond, and then made a big move – in partnership with a new class of owner.

Michael Dell established his original PCs Limited business in 1984 when he was at the University of Texas. In many ways, his story mirrors the success of latter-day digital entrepreneurs. Already a visionary, Dell and his close colleagues were disruptive innovators from the very beginning. To use the language of Clayton Christiansen, they invented a new business model that disrupted the upstream and downstream "value networks" of the incumbent personal computer brands, such as IBM, Compaq and others.

As with most disruptors, Dell started at the commodity end of the PC business, building IBM-compatible machines assembled from stock components. Largely ignored by IBM and other established PC manufacturers in the early 1980s, in 1985 Dell then produced its own computer to its own design, the Turbo. The disruptive innovation was to advertise directly to consumers, largely through specialist computer magazines, and to offer

PCs custom-assembled according to a selection of options – initiating the company's "configure-to-order" philosophy.

Resisting the lure of large distribution deals with Wal-Mart and other large retailers, Dell stuck with a direct-to-consumer model, which gained momentum when it launched its internet site in 1997. Here was a simple interface where mainly computer-savvy customers could build their own powerful computers, adding multiple features meeting their individual needs, and having them delivered in days. This customer group knew what it was doing, so costly technical support was not needed beyond online community advice.

While the prices of standard industry products to consumers were going down, Dell's average selling price was going up. Operating costs made up only 10% of Dell's $35 billion revenues in 2002, as compared with 21% at Hewlett Packard, for example. And Dell attained the number-one ranking for PC reliability, customer service and technical support. The "new kid on the block" had now fully disrupted the established PC market. Classic established brands such as Compaq, Gateway, Packard Bell and AST struggled and were eventually sold. Even after the merger of Compaq with Hewlett Packard, the new, larger combined entity struggled and it was not long before Dell had retained its top spot.

The serial disruptor struck again. In the mid-1990s, Dell expanded into the servers market. But rather than building proprietary technology like IBM, Hewlett Packard and Compaq, Dell innovated by running Windows NT on standard Intel chips. Its high-performance servers were significantly cheaper and rapidly built market position. In 2001, Dell passed Compaq as the top provider of Intel-based servers, with 31% of the market.

The high-water mark for Dell's stock price was $62 in July 2005. But by June 2006, the stock traded 40% lower. The next ten years were difficult. The PC market had matured. The cost advantage of Dell's ultra-lean manufacturing model disappeared as competitors like Hewlett Packard and Acer responded. Dell found itself "drifting to the bottom" as the market changed – Dell had comparatively less scope to up-sell upgrades and was now selling a greater proportion of inexpensive PCs, leading to eroding margins. The direct-sell channel became a disadvantage, as consumers either wanted to go to specialty stores for advice, or to Wal-Mart for rock-bottom prices. Lack of retail presence made it difficult to sell new products such as notebooks, flat-screen TVs and MP3 players. Service levels and brand reputation plummeted.

The advantages of its original disruptive model – direct sales, component assembly and supply chain efficiencies – had become obstacles in the changing market and Dell had not responded. Delivering individual PCs to customer specifications from the US was no longer as efficient or competitive as compared with high-volume Asian manufacturers. Costs of reinventing the value networks, investing in R&D and adding new products became difficult to justify in an environment of declining sales and margins. In 2007, Dell was forced into a programme of restructuring and painful downsizing, coupled with a diversification of the company's products. To make things worse, Dell's PC world was hit by the growing popularity of Apple's iPad, smartphones and tablet computers, which drove down profits further.

Dell had been trying to offset the inexorable decline in the PC business by investing in new sectors: the enterprise market with servers (already well-established), networking, software and services. Dell moved positively into services, acquiring Perot Systems for $3.9 billion in 2009. Further large acquisitions followed later – for example, Quest, bought for $2.7 billion. But by 2013, it was clear that Dell was unable to convince the markets that it could prosper and make a successful transition to a post-PC world, even with this diversification. The stock price continued to decline.

BIG MOVE 1: GOING PRIVATE

In 2013, Michael Dell, now back with the company after an absence of several years, and his management team were conscious of the forces of disruption and were suffering from an acute case of the stuckness predicament, as described in chapter 8:

- The existing PC core market could not be the backbone of a sustainable business in the future
- The orthodox organizational form of a public company seemed to restrict Dell's ability to respond nimbly to the rapid changes occurring
- The markets' requirement for short-term performance, while at the same time demonstrating a long-term sustainable plan, was impossible to achieve
- Given the decline in market confidence, investments in R&D and acquisitions could not be financed from capital markets
- Morale and prospects were at rock bottom.

On the other hand, the Dell brand (both corporate and personal) remained strong. Customer loyalty and affection remained. There were attractive businesses lurking within the enterprise. The company's employees had a wealth of knowledge, skill and experience in the computer hardware, servers and services markets.

In February 2013, the Dell board announced that it had agreed to a $24.4 billion leveraged buy-out deal with Silver Lake Partners, one of the world's largest technology private equity and leveraged buy-out firms, and that it would be delisting its shares from the NASDAQ and Hong Kong stock exchanges, taking the company private. The transaction closed in October 2013. At the time, it was the largest technology firm buy-out ever.

Seven percent reductions in manpower were implemented in the following year or so. With the freedom of action provided by his new owners, Dell was able to make some progress. At the November 2015 EMEA Solutions Conference in Vienna, Michael Dell, still the CEO, was able to report that the company had experienced 11 successive quarters gaining share in the client business and that it was also gaining share in the server business. He claimed that customer loyalty was at record levels and that the company was innovating more than ever – it had filed 27% more patents so far in 2015 than it had in 2014.

BIG MOVE 2: ACQUISITION OF EMC

Back in 2002, Dell's then-president and COO had wanted to fix the company's dependency on the PC market by acquiring EMC Corporation, a Massachusetts-based data storage company, but this had been blocked by chairman and CEO Michael Dell.

At the beginning of October 2015, now privately-held Dell announced that it had agreed to pay $67 billion for EMC, using a huge $50 billion of leveraged debt to finance the deal. This price set another new record as the biggest-ever takeover in technology history.

In one expensive bound, the merger of Dell with EMC will (they claim) be able to compete head-to-head with IBM and Hewlett Packard, offering a broad capability to customers facing technology-driven disruption. In its announcement, Dell claims that the combined companies will have "leadership positions in servers, storage, virtualization and PCs and strong capabilities in the fastest-growing areas of our industry, including digital transformation, software defined data centre, hybrid cloud, converged infrastructure, mobile and security."

The deal has been met with a mixture of bewilderment and hostility in the industry, as much about the strategy, the timing of the deal in the cycle, the price and the financing. But we need not be concerned about that here. I am less interested in the rightness of the deal than in the strategy adopted to react to disruption and to escape denial.

INGREDIENTS FOR A BIG MOVE STRATEGY: DOING A DELL

The Dell story throws up the following ingredients for a successful big move:
- Acceptance of the reality of disruption and that capital markets have lost faith
- A resolve to "get cracking"
- Escape from the constraining clutches of the shareholder capitalistic model
- A backer with nous and deep pockets
- A top team with a vision for long-term success
- An execution plan.

The inquiry into denial in part 2 of this book highlighted the limited appetite, let alone freedom of action, that top teams in established enterprises espousing the orthodox organizational form have to deal with radically in disruptive innovation.

In the Dell example, going private was a precondition for doing something. Capital markets had lost faith in the management's ability to improve earnings and to implement a strategy for reducing dependency on PCs. At this point, the company was either condemned to die the "death of a thousand cuts," or to find a different ownership structure and source of financial backing.

Top teams and boards, informed as necessary by conversations with major investing institutions, need a sanguine answer to a fundamental question: will the markets back the existing management team to pursue a fundamental transformation into a new business arena, which will be less exposed to disruptive innovation from new business models?

If the answer is yes, and an established enterprise is in a position where the capital markets have not yet lost faith, then there remains scope for it to transform its business model and reposition itself in a market with less risk of disruption, with or without a big move, drawing on the support of equity and debt markets.

There are many successes that one can point to. IBM achieved a fundamental repositioning of its business in its move from hardware manufacturer to solutions provider in the 1990s. In the 1970s, Otis, the elevator company, switched its business model from selling elevators to servicing them and providing "building access" solutions. Madsbjerg and Rasmussen (Madsbjerg, 2014) describe in their book, *Moment of Clarity*, how companies as diverse as Lego, Adidas, Intel and Samsung were able to move forward with the support of capital markets in the refocusing of their businesses once they had their "moment of clarity" about what the beneficiaries of their products – their customers – really wanted and needed, as opposed to the assumptions about human behaviours that the companies had had previously.

These companies will still need to change their business model from "pipes" to a business model with "platform" features, and make moves to transform the climate for inspiring their employees – but they have a chance of survival as quoted enterprises within their more sustainable business arena, at least in the short term.

If the answer is no, then going private is a *sine qua non* for successful reinvention and transformation – as was the case with Dell.

THE CASE FOR PRIVATE EQUITY AS A NEW OWNER

I was saddened to read last year of the death of Jim Slater. He had a big influence on me during my formative business years in the late 1960s and 1970s. On this side of the "pond," Jim was a trailblazer for the future private equity industry. He developed a fearsome reputation as an "asset stripper," investing in underperforming firms and forcing management to dispose of unproductive assets. In an interview in 1992, he said, "I don't deny asset stripping, although the phrase is used as a smear, usually by spineless people who cannot manage their companies. If a firm had assets stripped, it means they have not been properly used." (The Daily Telegraph, 2015) Another time, he is reported to have said, "It's like a knife and butter. And we're the knife." These quotes capture the aura of the public man.

I had a sneaky respect for Jim Slater, but felt somewhat guilty about it. People close to him found Jim to be self-effacing, "normal," and loyal to his family and friends. I recall an evening in a London pub when I was "torn off a strip" by a group of friends when I timidly tried to explain that he was fulfilling a necessary role of transferring assets from the inefficient to the efficient and that this was good for the economy over the long term. Coming from a middle-class home steeped in Christian values, I was programmed to think first and foremost of the unfairness to those losing their jobs and how Jim was enriching himself at others' expense - what Prime Minister Edward Heath, in another context, later called "the unacceptable face of capitalism." Experiencing the bloated inefficiency of British industry at that time, I saw the need for radical surgery to ensure long-term survival.

In later life, I became more intimately familiar with the private equity industry, in conducting due diligence in major deals, working with new management teams and new private equity owners to implement "100-day plans" and as chairman of a private equity funded business, which required turnaround. I was by no means attracted to the rampant greed I saw around me, nor by the transient philosophy of restructuring an acquired business for sale. But I experienced first-hand remarkable reinvention and reawakening stories – for example, a sleepy engineering division treated as an unloved orphan by its big-brand parent, acquired, stripped down to the bone, repositioned into another sector, combined with an acquisition, and achieving a remarkable turnaround to profitability. And then of course it was sold at a massive premium to another conglomerate – but now with highly motivated and productive employees adding real value for customers and new owners alike.

GET ON THE FRONT FOOT – FIND THE RIGHT PARTNER

I do not want to come across as an apologist for private equity, but merely point out that, as was the case with Dell, the right partner can be the precondition for survival for a management team of a quoted enterprise experiencing the powerlessness of the stuckness predicament, described in chapter 8.

Private equity "predators" will come knocking at your door whether you like it or not, particularly if your share price is languishing or declining. From my experience, such firms vary considerably in expertise and philosophy, let alone human values. Some are looking purely for a quick exercise in downsizing for short-term cash generation needed to repay high levels of leveraged debt – and then an exit through sale to an industry buyer or by stock market flotation. Others are very professional, looking more long term, and can bring real expertise, human and financial resources to help with the repositioning of the business away from disruptive forces, better positioned for long-term survival.

My message to boards and top management teams is, "Get on the front foot!" This metaphor comes from games of cricket and baseball – if you are on the back foot, you are nearly always defensive, forced to react to the ball and circumstances. If you are on the front foot, you have the initiative and can influence things. As Jim Slater had no shame in admitting, there will be casualties in jobs lost both with employees and suppliers, but the right partner can help with suitable separation packages and retraining initiatives. Otherwise, the right deal will be a win-win – existing owners will achieve a significant price premium and the new owners will have the prospect of the creation of significant new value. Management and staff will participate in a share of this, in most cases.

A LAST WORD ON DELL

I am not privy to what happened in the case of Silver Lake and Michael Dell – whether Michael was on the back foot or the front foot, nor who came knocking first. I am not surprised by the humming and ha-ing going on in the industry and trade press about the planned EMC deal. As the UK Chancellor Denis Healey is reported to have said in another context: "If the pips are squeaking, then the juice is flowing." Two professional organizations have a clear vision of what the combined business can achieve and have significant financial "skin in the game." I, for one, wish them luck.

CHAPTER 12
DISRUPTING YOURSELF

INCREMENTAL VERSUS DISRUPTIVE INNOVATION

In 1998, some colleagues and I were spending a weekend in a swanky hotel in deepest Yorkshire, hosting a "blue sky thinking" workshop with 30 or so senior people from major European consumer and manufacturing companies. There was a loose and informal agenda. We talked a lot about "ideation" – how to conceive innovative ideas and transform them into new products.

Most of these executives came from research and development (R&D) or new product development (NPD). For the most part, they had an engineering or scientific background. They were incremental innovators. These people focus on today's business model, today's product sets, today's processes and today's customers. They are pragmatic people who know that they must work within the realities of their organization and its constraints. They know that product extensions, packaging innovations, and improvements to the website, for example, will make it through the system. They are proud to weed out fanciful ideas. They are important assets to the company in its current business model and should be encouraged to continue with their creative innovations. But they are not disruptive innovators.

This doesn't stop them from being frustrated with their lot. "We had to set up a 'skunkworks' to get anything done, otherwise the business would have smothered it," said Nathalie, the director of a well-known, fast-moving consumer goods (FMCG) company. This contribution triggered a lively debate about how it was impossible to do anything creative within their organizations because of the inability of top management to understand the creative process and its desire to impose unrealistic budgeting and reporting constraints. "They have frequent cot deaths and then grieve interminably about them," I remember as a particularly graphic contribution.

There were also a few executives from strategy, business development and marketing. These people have a mandate for "thinking out of the box," exploring "greenfield opportunities" and you will also find them in the executive suite. They are trying to find the "silver bullet" with the potential to transform the company and which will kill off competition. At this gathering, it was obvious that these MBA types were considered a breed apart, barely tolerated for the most part by the R&D and NPD pragmatists. "Let them have their say," the latter seemed to be thinking, without taking this non-engineering approach very seriously.

There were no flashes of insight from this meeting, as I can recall, although good contacts were made and networks were strengthened.

Neither of the groups represented at this pleasant gathering and their respective approaches will produce disruptive innovations – and this was the "elephant in the room," the frustration that triggered the graphic metaphors. The R&D and NPD folk will help rejuvenate the existing business model within its current value networks – a valuable function. The MBA types will dream up new business diversification ideas, but few will make it through to reality, since they must pass the tests of discounted cash flow and resource allocation.

A few reminders about disruptive innovations as developed earlier in this book:

- They recast the business model adopted by established enterprises, applying new, usually simpler and cheaper upstream and downstream value networks (new manufacturing, distribution and customer access approaches)
- They focus on things customers didn't think they could want or need (cheap point-to-point travel, a device that is both a phone and a computer, readily accessible music without need for a specific device to listen to it on)
- They may appear wacky and impractical to all involved at the beginning
- They initially appear unthreatening to established enterprises, serving what seems to be a small market
- They can rapidly invade the core business of established enterprises
- Many will fail
- They are nearly always created by start-ups working in nontraditional organizational environments; but they can scale fast.

Of course, you will point out that large companies can do disruptive innovation. Companies like Apple, Microsoft, Amazon, Google and Dell have grown spectacularly though serial disruptive innovations. In nearly all cases, however, this is because they started life as disruptive innovators themselves and the inspirational visionary founder(s) guarded the disruptive innovation thinking around themselves. They established structures, processes and systems to allow the innovations to flourish and get deployed. They did not have the legacy infrastructure, systems, processes and mindsets that most established enterprises in traditional industries have inherited and have difficulty in shaking off. And they were successful, so shareholders were happy to let them get on with it.

Steve Jobs, Bill Gates, Andy Grove, Larry Page, Sergey Brin, Jeff Bezos and Michael Dell ensured that the DNA of disruptive innovation was instilled in their businesses and became a lens through which they and the company looked at the world. As we saw in the previous chapter, when Dell entered the servers market, it was to disrupt it with a different business model, not simply a diversification into a complementary business area. During the periods when Steve Jobs left Apple and Michael Dell left Dell, the companies tended to revert to an orthodox mindset – diversification through acquisition and synergies, and the disruptive innovation mindset was somewhat diminished – for example, when Dell acquired Perot Systems to enter the services market. The disruptive innovation mindset returned when the inspirational founders returned to pick up the reins again.

THE "DISRUPT YOURSELF" MINDSET AND STRATEGY

Remember that I suggested at the beginning of the previous chapter that there are two fundamental steps needed, whatever else an established enterprise does, to move beyond denial and to survive in a disrupted world:
- Reach a state of acceptance with a resolve to "get cracking"
- Build your platform-compatible business model with "platform" features.

I suggested that these are the *sine qua non* requirements for the long-term survival of your company. After all, if you cannot recognize reality and the need to do something serious about it, there is no point in moving further. And unless you change your business model away from a "pipes" view to a "platform-enabled ecosystem" view, then there is little hope.

So our starting point is that the board, top team and major players throughout the organization "get it," are ready to "get cracking" and that you have launched a fully-resourced programme to transfer your infrastructure, systems and processes from "pipes" to a "platform." So a lot is already happening – awareness of transformational change is getting embedded.

Here are some things you can do to lay the groundwork and put in the pipe work for a successful "disrupt yourself" posture (*see Figure 14*):

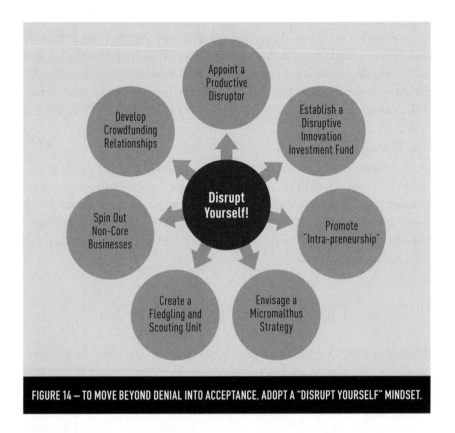

FIGURE 14 – TO MOVE BEYOND DENIAL INTO ACCEPTANCE, ADOPT A "DISRUPT YOURSELF" MINDSET.

APPOINT A PRODUCTIVE DISRUPTOR TO THE EXECUTIVE COMMITTEE

Disruptive innovation (not just digital transformation) needs to be represented at the highest executive level. A recent survey conducted by Forrester Research demonstrated that all C-level executives in major enterprises claim to be digitally aware (Gill, 2014). But will they prioritize digital ventures outside incremental innovations? Are they really committed to the idea of investing outside the firm in early stage businesses, which may one day threaten the company? Will employees lower down the pyramid really believe that the company has embraced the digital world and the need for disruptive innovation unless they see a credible person doing innovative things in the executive committee?

While the board and the whole executive committee need to buy into the notion of a "disrupt yourself" posture, the CEO and top team need a productive disruptor at the top table. An executive who, according to the Russell Reynolds report cited earlier, is 34% more innovative in his or her thinking than peers, 32% more prepared to be disruptive within the organization, 23% bolder in leadership, 21% more socially adept and 16% more determined (Russell Reynolds, 2015). Such a person will be drawn from a different gene pool of background, education and career path and will have a different world view from the other executives. He or she has a real chance to enrich the DNA in the executive suite, make sure that the move to a "platform" business gets resources and priority, and ensure that the "disrupt yourself" initiatives described below do not get diluted over time. Such a person helps to engender belief.

ESTABLISH A DISRUPTIVE INNOVATION INVESTMENT FUND

These days, I spend part of my time with Elixirr, where I am an associate partner. At first sight, Elixirr is just a fast-growing and successful consulting firm; but the firm has committed itself to innovating in the consulting market. If it is to be credible in exposing clients to the innovation of entrepreneurial start-ups, the firm needs to be entrepreneurial in fact as well as in intent. A few years back, the partners established Elixirr Capital, which invests in innovative technological businesses. Most investments come through The Pitch, a process modelled on the *Dragons Den* and *Shark Tank* TV concepts. Entrepreneurs both from within the company and from employees' personal networks pitch their business start-up proposals to the partner "dragons". If successful, the partners of the firm commit to fund the start-up and to provide ongoing support to the investee companies. In this way, Elixirr walks the talk about being entrepreneurial and reinventing consulting – consequently, it attracts and retains the best talent, which has positive spinoff for the rest of this people-based business.

You can do something similar. Get the board to commit a significant sum to your disruptive innovation fund – but give it a better name that means something to your company! Given the vital importance to the firm, would 50% of what you dedicate to R&D be too much funding to commit?

Set up the fund as a separate venture outside the company, with its own articles and governance in line with industry norms. Put your CEO and the productive disruptor on the investment committee alongside external appointees. Persuade the board and your finance director to treat the fund in the books as a long-term asset class labelled high-risk/high-reward. You can focus its objectives on your customers, their ecosystem of networks and needs and on innovations with the potential to affect your business. In fact, pretty much everything!

Promote your readiness to prioritize funding of innovative start-ups sourced from within the company. I suspect that you will be staggered by the number of quality proposals that will come forward from within the company. There will be people who feel emboldened to put forward business ideas that they may have been working on in their own time, and that they thought would be scorned by the company. It is not surprising that many new ideas will come from within – after all, the best-placed people to understand new opportunities are those who are in day-to-day contact with customers, suppliers, technology providers and so on.

Your fund will make seed investments in potentially disruptive innovations. When you see businesses that could disrupt your core business model and value networks, then participate in further rounds of funding to promote growth. *But resist the temptation to bring the company back into the main business.* You let the bird continue to fly with its own wings. You are effectively owners of a disruptive business, which could replace much or all of what you do now. So do not smother it at birth.

PROMOTE "INTRAPRENEURSHIP"

Create a culture of "intrapreneurship" within the organization by supporting employees to incubate their own ideas and create their own projects. Google famously encourages employees to spend some of their time on their own projects without predefined guidelines, while others such as eBay, Deloitte, Barclays and Elixirr actively encourage employees to "seek forgiveness rather than permission" if they have a great idea. Do something similar!

CREATE A FLEDGLING AND SCOUTING UNIT

Establish a fledging and scouting unit. Its role is as its name implies – to nurture and to give early-stage businesses the skills and the oxygen to leave the nest and fly. And to persistently scout in the online world, in innovation centres such as the Silicon Valleys around the world, keeping track of interesting start-ups and growing businesses, and keeping close to the speciality venture capital funds, which follow innovative technologies and management teams.

The productive disruptor C-Suite executive should take direct responsibility for the unit, in addition to other responsibilities. Not only reacting to and nurturing investment opportunities coming to the fund, this unit will also be actively seeking to associate with innovative companies that could innovate in adjacent areas outside the core businesses of the company.

As and when timely, the unit may put proposals to the executive committee to acquire all or part of the share capital of qualifying early-stage businesses – such businesses to be kept separate with their own Digital Age Disruptive organizational form (see next chapter).

SPIN OUT NON-CORE BUSINESSES

There will be business units or services that are important to your value networks, but which up to now have not merited disposal. Actively seek them out! Some of them, suitably enfranchised and given freedom outside the company, may have the potential to become disruptive innovations to your business model. You should spin them out as separate businesses, preferably with the people who understand the activity and with passion for it as the management team.

Provide them with a contract for services, or some such offering, to make it easier for them to arrange external equity funding, such as crowdfunding, and encourage debt-funding instruments so that you can avoid consolidation in your accounts. Keep an eye on them!

DEVELOP CROWDFUNDING RELATIONSHIPS

Crowdfunding is moving from its heady, rather chaotic adolescence into a more mature phase, which can be useful to you as you adopt a "disrupt yourself" mindset. Although you do not need the money, you could benefit from potential access to disruptive ideas, and from testing of your own innovations, which may have been orphaned in your organization for years.

Indiegogo is an example of a crowdfunding partner moving from simply arranging funding (often to a couple of guys with a good idea and video editing skills) to adding value to start-ups on its platform. They are looking to build a new community of experienced corporate partners to use their crowdfunding platform as a test bed; and it will partner with manufacturers and distributors that can help bring Indiegogo-funded products to market.

Other crowdfunding platforms may well move in this direction too – so keeping aware of these possibilities will be a key role for your productive disruptor and his or her colleagues.

ENVISAGE A MICROMALTHUS (CHILD-EATS-MOTHER) STRATEGY AND ENDGAME

Yes, there is an example in the animal kingdom of a species evolving by the child eating its mother! So I am using the tiny, wood-boring beetle, *Micromalthus debilis*, as my metaphor for a possible endgame an established enterprise might have in its own strategy for survival.

Most *Micromalthus* beetles are female, so the propagation of healthy males is vital for survival. Once a female beetle has laid a rare male egg (by virgin birth), and the instant the male larva has hatched, it plunges its head back into its mother, and proceeds to devour the contents of her body. Once it has finished consuming its hapless mother, the cannibalistic off-spring will go through a series of development mutations until culminating in a winged adult male! So a *Micromalthus* approach it is! Not immediately at birth, but part of a long-term endgame!

Let us look at a few cases where a *Micromalthus* endgame might be envisageable.

MBANK

If you go to the website of BRE Bank, a long-established traditional bank in Poland (part of the Commerzbank Group), you will find a nice letter from the president, Cezary Stypułkowski, explaining that BRE Bank is shortly to merge its different operations under the mBank brand.

What is less obvious is that this is much more than a rebranding and efficiency story. It is a child-eats-mother story.

Forgive me, but BRE Bank was a boring bricks-and-mortar bank with an extensive branch network, classic product offerings, and frankly pretty mediocre customer service. The top team had the vision back in 2000 to reinvent banking in Poland by creating a best-of-the-best online bank. So, BRE Band launched mBank in 2000 as a pure-play online bank start-up. The circumstances were favourable for creating a digital bank: the creaking banking infrastructure post-communism needed replacement; telco infrastructure was developing rapidly and there was rapid mobile phone adoption; and, a young generation was ready for new technologies and e-commerce experiences.

Starting from nothing, mBank's client base has grown organically with 4.6 million retail clients and almost 18,000 corporate customers at the end of 2014. How has it done this? Basically by allowing a great entrepreneurial team the freedom to grow the business without interference. After a significant migration in June 2013 to an app/browser/multi-interface platform, mBank now offers one of the best online banking experiences anywhere – a congenial, intuitive front-end that beats established banks hollow, offering a full range of products and services delivered seamlessly online, using many of the disruptive innovations described in chapter 2 of this book. Features include one-time PIN-enabled login and transaction authentication; a 30-second loan option enabled by automatic credit scoring and clearing through a revised payments engine and backup architecture; a smart transaction search engine; a "messages with cash" feature using social media; a personal financial management tool incorporating "safe to spend" alerts based upon self-set financial management criteria; one-touch access to online expertise by video or phone 24/7; and, importantly, an open API services architecture to extend the value proposition – to insurance, for example.

Online mBank has indeed been a startling disruptive innovation for retail banking, and is the obvious future for the BRE parent – hence the reverse merger. The "online first" banking model will drive the culture, platform and value networks of the new merged bank, although the full effects will no doubt take time to become apparent. In a few years, the child will have fully digested the mother.

AVIS / ZIPCAR

There are many other potential *Micromalthus* scenarios out there. Take the familiar rental car company, Avis, which includes the Budget and Zipcar brands. In 2011, Avis Budget was able to acquire Avis Europe plc, reuniting the US-based parent with the licensee for Europe, the Middle East, Africa and Asia. Now was a chance to innovate the creaking infrastructure and customer service offering for the mainly business traveller.

In January 2013, Avis acquired Zipcar Inc. for $500 million, a 49% premium to the car-sharing-network operator's NASDAQ price, but a 32% discount to Zipcar's $18 IPO price.

Zipcar went public in April 2011 and shot as high as $31.50 in its debut. But the shares never closed above $30, and had languished below $10 since the company posted second-quarter results in August 2012.

Zipcar has been a disruptive innovation to the rental car industry. Focusing initially on students in residence halls on university campuses, it offered a convenient hourly rental product – filling a need gap between public transportation and using one's own car. It had expanded fast, broadening its focus to young and urban customers and had signed up more than 760,000 members since its founding in 2000. But it had struggled to post a consistent profit. The deal would vault Avis ahead of its peers in the niche hourly rental market, which had grown to nearly a $400 million business in the US, Avis said.

"I've been somewhat dismissive of car sharing in the past," Avis chief executive Ron Nelson said during a conference call. "But what I've come to realize is that car sharing, particularly on the scale that Zipcar has achieved and will achieve, is complementary to our traditional business."

There were obvious synergies to be achieved in car procurement and that alone could justify the acquisition and the price paid. But could Avis be preparing itself for a fully disrupted rental world? Could Zipcar become a *Micromalthus* story? After all, it has the platform, ecosystem and culture to do so!

IAG/VUELING

In April 2013, International Airlines Group (IAG) acquired control of the low-cost carrier (LCC) Vueling. This acquisition was an inheritance from the acquisition of Iberia by IAG, also the owner of British Airways. But it quickly became clear that IAG was determined to keep Vueling separate from Iberia and British Airways, allowing Vueling to continue to disrupt and facilitate the much-needed restructuring of Iberia. Willie Walsh, IAG's CEO, stated in April 2013, "Vueling will operate as a stand-alone entity in IAG Group."

As compared with other pure-play LCCs such as Ryanair, Vueling has long developed a hybrid product, which seems well suited to a continued independent role in IAG – a basic LCC offering, and a premium offering focusing on business travellers at the front of the plane. And it had developed a hybrid reservation platform that encourages direct booking, but also gives travel agents the ability to book for their business clients. But it has a significantly lower cost structure – salaries for pilots and cabin crew, in-airport handling fees, overhead – and can now benefit from the bulk buying muscle of IAG in fuel, insurance and aircraft.

Does IAG simply see Vueling as a Trojan horse for forcing through fundamental reform to the inefficient practices and high cost structure of a legacy airline group conceived in a different era? Or, as and when the cycle of profitability slips and the legacy model is visibly no longer sustainable (the Sabena scenario), could Vueling become a *Micromalthus* scenario?

CONCLUSION

Disruptive innovations to your business model and the value networks that sustain them will happen. New digital technologies open up limitless possibilities: they could be an existential threat; you can't start them easily yourself (your whole way of behaving will only allow incremental innovation – à la Clay Christiansen); you will smother them if you try to manage them according to orthodox business rules; but, you must do them; and, you must take steps to compete in the disruptive world.

A "disrupt yourself" mindset and action plan is vital. Take the suggestions made here seriously, as part of your post-denial response to the new reality.

CHAPTER 13

BUILDING A DIGITAL AGE DISRUPTIVE (DAD) ORGANIZATION

Whether your company makes a big move, takes "disrupt yourself" steps, or simply hunkers down to ride out the storm, you need to take steps to make your organization better able to accommodate the changes we have been looking at: employees with different lifestyles, values and aspirations; the creep of machines replacing people; the challenge to core activities from the actions of disruptive business models; and so on.

You need to evolve to become a Digital Age Disruptive (DAD) organization. Making such an organizational evolution, combined with your move on the journey toward a "platform" model (a constant requirement for all, as explored in chapter 10) should enable you to survive all but the most fundamental and determined disruptions.

What are we looking for as you move toward becoming more like a pure-play Digital Age Disruptive (DAD) organization?

- A clear mandate from the top
- An organization with less dominant hierarchy and a flatter structure
- A leaner, more agile business
- A place that attracts and retains talent
- A company that embraces technology change.

LESSONS FROM A SUCCESSFUL DAD – BUURTZORG

Buurtzorg (meaning "neighbourhood care" in Dutch) is one of the 12 companies that Frederic Laloux looked at in detail in his book, *Reinventing Organizations* (Laloux, 2014). In the context of the theme of this book, I have labelled this kind of mode of operation a Digital Age Disruptive (DAD) organization.

Buurtzorg has fundamentally disrupted the provision of care in the home, as much by its new organizational form as by its new business model. The home page of Buurtzorg's website describes what they are about:

"Buurtzorg Nederland was founded in 2006 by Jos de Blok and a small team of professional nurses who were dissatisfied with the delivery of health care by traditional home-care organizations in the Netherlands. Together they decided to create a new model of patient-centred care focused on facilitating and maintaining independence and autonomy for the individual for as long as possible."

"I believe in client-centred care, with nursing that is independent and collaborative" said Jos de Blok, director and CEO, Buurtzorg Nederland.

"The community-based nurse should have a central role – after all, they know best how they can support specific circumstances for the client." (Buurtzorg, 2016)

Jos de Blok, himself a nurse, believes in an empowered nurse-led team approach, as well as an empowered patient. He believes most patients can be encouraged to participate together with their Buurtzorg nurse in finding solutions to their home-care needs, and that many of these solutions can be found right in the community.

What started as a team of four nurses in 2006 had grown to nearly 8,000 nurses by 2014, with teams in the Netherlands, Sweden, Japan and now the United States. A 2010 Ernst & Young report documented savings of roughly 40% to the Dutch health-care system. A 2012 KPMG case study found:

"Essentially, the program empowers nurses (rather than nursing assistants or cleaners) to deliver all the care that patients need. And while this has meant higher costs per hour, the result has been fewer hours in total. Indeed, by changing the model of care, Buurtzorg has accomplished a 50% reduction in hours of care, improved quality of care and raised work satisfaction for their employees."

Further down on the home page, Buurtzorg lays out what distinguishes it from other home-care organizations:

- The team approach allows for the best solutions to promote independence and quality of life, and allows nurses the autonomy to practice to their highest level of training.
- All Buurtzorg nurses are responsible for promoting and providing outstanding care. They focus not only on current needs, but also on preventing future problems.
- The Buurtzorg nurse acts as "a navigator" for the patient and family, helping them find the most relevant and innovative solutions to receiving the care they need at home.
- Nurses are supported by a simple and streamlined organization with modern IT technology to facilitate "real time" information that is directly connected to the care process and reduces administrative overhead.
- Buurtzorg nurses provide licensed, professional care in accordance with the highest national and international professional standards, which are evidence-based and closely monitored.

In his excellent book, Laloux goes into great detail an how Buurtzorg and the other for-profit and not-for-profit organizations he studied have put in place processes to allow a non-hierarchical, purpose-drive organization to thrive. Buurtzorg now dominates home nursing provision and is astonishingly successful in every measure, including financially. And the Dutch health-care system has realized significant economies – a true win-win due to a productive disruptive innovation.

What was the essence of the Buurtzorg formula, which Laloux has distilled out of his analysis of the 12 case histories?

Self-management. The companies operate effectively, even at scale, within a system based upon peer relationships, without the need for hierarchy or consensus.

Wholeness. They create environments wherein employees are encouraged to bring their whole person to work, not just their rational selves. Employees do not park their emotional, intuitive and spiritual beings along with their cars when they arrive at work.

Evolutionary purpose. Members of these organizations espouse the sense of purpose of the organization, where it wants to go and what it wants to achieve. The company becomes almost like a living organism with a purpose of its own, which employees, customers and other stakeholders latch on to. This is what drives the company forward. Financial results are a fortunate (even inevitable) consequence, not a primary driver.

You might want to deny the relevance of the Buurtzorg story – nursing is not retail distribution, or whatever; or this was in the caring industry, not commerce; it was not-for-profit.

And you would be at least half right. Buurtzorg, and nearly all the firms Laloux examined, were organizations launched by a driven, inspirational leader or small team (or in the case of family businesses, restarted by a new family member).

Although Buurtzorg remains a private company, other examples described by Laloux thrived while they remained private under original leadership, but rapidly lost their sparkle when they went public or came under new management less sympathetic to the business model that had made them successful. It seems that what I am calling this new Digital Age Disruptive organizational model thrives in early-stage businesses or start-ups but struggles in large established enterprises.

But you are also half wrong! Once you and your board and executive committee have reached a state of acceptance with a determination to "get cracking" (chapter 8), and committed to the move to the "platform" posture described in chapter 9, there are things you can do to move purposefully toward a DAD organization and gain many of the benefits of a pure play such as Buurtzog.

You should not be discouraged that, even after your company's transition from an orthodox organizational paradigm, you will be unlikely to ever be able to a match the costs, agility and dynamism of a pure-play organization such as Buurtzorg – such is the overhang of legacy, including unionized labour and infrastructure. The journey will indeed be fraught with difficulty. However, a reinvented, revitalized organization combined with the strength of other parts of your legacy (brands, reputation, partnerships, laid-down investment), should make penetration by new disruptors less attractive and more difficult. Your company will be well placed to compete.

So, let us look at the things you can do (*see Figure 15*).

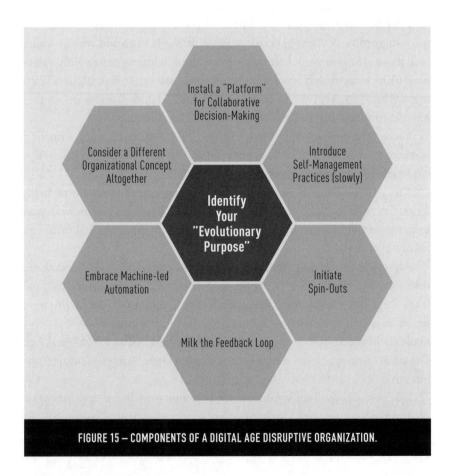

FIGURE 15 – COMPONENTS OF A DIGITAL AGE DISRUPTIVE ORGANIZATION.

CONSIDER A DIFFERENT ORGANIZATIONAL CONCEPT ALTOGETHER

Take a look at Holacracy. This is a concept of organization conceived in 2007 by Brian Robertson of Ternary Software, which replaces formal company hierarchies with a flatter structure consisting of self-managed "circles." In his book published in 2010, *Holacracy: The New Management System for a Rapidly Changing World* (Robertson, 2015), Robertson describes the principles and the practices of a Holacracy. You might want to evaluate whether the Holacracy ethos, methods and governance will work for you – 300 US companies have adopted the model, the most high-profile of which is the online shoe retailer Zappos, a billion-dollar company that began implementing Holacracy in 2013.

Proponents point out that Holacracy mirrors the sort of workflow software that emerged in the 1990s, and it is formalizing the informal way in which companies, particularly rapidly growing technology and digital companies, operate. It may not be for you, or pertinent to your industry and business, but do take a reasoned look.

GAIN INSTITUTIONAL VALIDATION – ADOPT A NEW LEGAL FRAMEWORK

Even if you gain your board's and shareholders' acceptance to move toward a DAD model, there is danger that the commitment will be temporary. As soon as the organization hits rough waters, which it will do in the disruptive world we have been talking about, owners and their board may well revert to type – pull back control and decision-making to the centre in the interest of immediate expediency. So it will be sensible to explore ways in which you might enshrine your commitment to a different style of organization not solely interested in enriching shareholders into the legal framework of your company – in the constitution or articles of association of the company, for example.

You might wish to look at the Holacracy Constitution. This lays out the core principles of this system, which shareholders and boards can sign up to and which thereafter becomes binding, even on future shareholders. Some legal blocking and tackling has been done to make the constitution conform to US corporate law. Not many companies have yet adopted the

Holacracy Constitution wholesale, but there is a framework there that aspiring DAD boards and executive teams may choose to draw upon.

Another model you could explore is the B-Corporation, which is a new form of corporate entity adopted in 30 US states. As distinct from a traditional C-Corporation, the directors and officers are required to consider the impact of their decisions not only on shareholders, but also on society and the environment. Not surprisingly in today's unreformed world, raising capital from shareholders has been difficult for B-Corporations, since shareholders are required to judge performance against social and environmental criteria, not only on shareholder value creation. More enlightened investors may see that there is no conflict – companies that are conscious of these societal factors may in fact become more attractive to customers and the new generations of talent, and higher shareholder returns may be the consequence.

In any event, even short of a new legally, enshrined framework, you may wish to draw up a document such as a charter or declaration of intentions as a reference point both outside and inside the organization – this is what we stand for. Such a move will help to engender belief.

EMBRACE MACHINE-LED AUTOMATION

One way to force through a flatter organizational structure is to embrace and accelerate the inevitable wave of machine-led automation inside the organization, which will make swathes of supervisory and middle management positions redundant (*See chapter 2*).

Even if your top executives are on board, the raft of senior and middle managers below the executive suite will be the big resisters – they will lose both hierarchical power and possibly even their jobs, as the logic of the new model plays out. After all, "turkeys do not vote for Christmas."

Start planning for this process now. Even the 50-year-old resisters will be able to engage, as will representatives of organized labour. Set up joint discussion groups, task forces or whatever. Involve your HR people in planning for retraining and attractive redundancy packages. Consider seed-funding employee-initiated start-ups, where appropriate, evaluated by your new fund (*see chapter 12*).

PROMOTE A CLIMATE OF PRODUCTIVE COLLABORATION

Many of the frustrations that confront employees of traditional enterprises, and repel the new generation attracted to the philosophies described by Fried and Hansson in their book, *Rework* (Hansson, 2010), relate to lack of communication and collaboration across organizational silos, resulting in "turf wars."

Behaviours that employees find natural at home, in the sports club or with their friends in the pub – listening, questioning, seeking real meaning – are checked at the door when they arrive at work. But it does not have to be so.

You should prioritize initiatives for people to relearn, as necessary, and to practice skills of productive encounters in the workplace as they tackle real tasks.

In 1999, I was invited by Theodore Taptiklis, of Storymaker Partners and the future author of *Unmanaging* (Taptiklis, 2007), to join a weekend gathering to experience the power of storytelling and "listening again." Ted and his colleagues had developed a simple mobile phone-based app for us to record stories and for us to be able to listen again and comment on what we heard. Interesting utterances were then to be tagged electronically for assembly into an archive of stories by theme. I remember telling a story of my first day at work, when I had been recruited to launch a new kind of hybrid strategy and corporate finance house in London back in 1985, the year of Big Bang deregulation of the British financial markets. I described to my conversation partner how I felt that first morning. What had I done? Why would anyone want to hire me or my new firm? How would I get a team together? Why had I left my cushy job in my previous firm? Listening again later to how I responded to her gentle prompts, I noticed changes of tone and mood, which reflected how I was now feeling about my risky investment into a dot-com venture. Angst, yes, but I seemed more sanguine. Perhaps I had moved on.

My conversation partner, Jane, told me how she was transitioning from a senior role in frontline nursing into a commissioning group for a major hospital trust. She felt that she was a "poacher turned gamekeeper," was feeling a bit disloyal, was wondering if she was doing right to leave her first love, nursing, and move into procurement management. As we listened again to our conversation, she heard things in the tone of voice that she found helpful – at least so she told me!

Why do I mention this? Because with the help of the right tools, you and your colleagues can rapidly engage with, relearn and practice skills that can lead to productive encounters in the workplace. Encourage all involved in a burning issue at work, across silos and those directly involved as practitioners, to use the frameworks and practices offered by organizations such as Storymaker. If you and they stick with it, working together in a collaborative way can become second nature and formal organizational charts fade into the background!

From the foundation of more productive encounters (both group and one-to-one), you will be well placed to add other processes that encourage the whole person to become present at work. Whether you develop your own processes, tap into concepts such as Mindfulness, or adopt other Storymaker tools and practices, being able to bring the whole potential of each individual to bear at work (and not just the part that the machine seems to accept) will be a key part of becoming a high-performing DAD – as Laloux's work shows. This is not "pink and fuzzy stuff," but a means to achieve outstanding performance – and therefore surely a priority.

INSTALL A PLATFORM FOR COLLABORATIVE DECISION-MAKING

In June 2009, Ted Taptiklis and I spent a long, congenial evening appreciating the unique atmosphere of the restaurant Chez Justine in the 11th arrondissement of Paris, imbibing good food and wine. Among the dishes and the wine glasses, we drew diagrams as we struggled to conceive a scalable online community for people in different times and places to discuss things that matter in a safe environment, and to reach purposeful decisions. This "Chez Justine moment," as we came to call it, was born out of the conviction that following the financial crash that we were living through, new ways of making informed decisions involving widespread voices would be clamoured for, and the internet offered an ideal platform. And that none of the emerging social media networks provided what was required.

A few false dawns came as we took the concept forward to various parties. No spark to ignite the idea at that point.

As it happened, on the other side of the world, in New Zealand, a bunch of brilliant technologists, social entrepreneurs and activists were onto the same idea. It took the Occupy Wall Street movement in 2011 to be the trigger for launch. Here were people from all walks of life and backgrounds in different parts of the world wanting to be heard by likeminded people, not just to protest, but also to make constructive proposals for a new economic system. They needed an effective, inclusive way to make decisions.

Loomio sparked to life. The founders set out to build a scalable tool that would provide the opportunity for people to be heard (or read), and to give them an easy way to make good decisions together, wherever they were. Now Loomio is used in 95 countries, has been translated into 33 languages and has enabled more than 20,000 groups to make more than 30,000 decisions. Groups range from political parties to social enterprises and corporations, large and small.

Loomio, or something like it, can become the platform for your people, wherever they are, to have their voice heard, and to participate in collective, inclusive decision-making. The online Loomio tool involves three stages, as explained on their website.

1. ***Talk things through.*** You can start a discussion on any topic and bring in diverse views from the ecosystem relating to the topic – for example, those involved in all silos within your company, but also interested parties from outside – customers, suppliers, regulators. The group shares diverse perspectives and develops ideas together.

2. ***Build agreement.*** Anyone can propose a course of action. People can agree, abstain, disagree or block – so you can see how everyone feels and why.

3. ***Decide together.*** The group develops a proposal together so that it works for everyone. Every decision has a clear deadline, so you always get a clear outcome. Compromises and "lowest common denominator" outcomes rarely arise.

Imagine the positive impact that a tool such as Loomio could have on your new organization – fewer interminable meetings, less conflict, real decision-making and follow-through, all with full collaborative input from all involved.

INTRODUCE SELF-MANAGEMENT PRACTICES (SLOWLY)

As productive conversation practices and collaborative decision-making take root, you can progress to gradual introduction of self-management practices. You can plan for their phased introduction, for example, by department where there is an enthusiastic group who "get it." You could set up a Loomio group to reach inclusive decisions on where to go next, and to what degree – communal accountability for results and self-budgeting, for example, as a first step.

Remember that younger employees, and people lower down in the pyramid, will tend to warm to the idea of self-management quickly. They will relish being heard and having freedom to shape their work as they think appropriate. On the other hand, most senior and middle managers are likely to see the introduction of self-management as a threat. They will lose power and their jobs may even be threatened if their function disappears, either as a natural by-product of the process, or from the trend to machine-led automation. So one-to-one, authentic consideration of each person's position and concerns will be vital.

INITIATE SPIN-OUTS

As discussed in the previous chapter, parts of your company's business – noncore businesses, like service activities, for example – will better thrive with the dead hand of the orthodox public company's stuckness predicament removed. They may nevertheless be important to you, and not candidates for outright divestment. Spin them out, preferably financed by debt instruments so that you can avoid consolidation in your accounts. Give them the freedom to operate in different forms – why not as cooperatives? But certainly as Buurtzorg-like DADs.

IDENTIFY AND FOCUS ON YOUR "EVOLUTIONARY PURPOSE"

I recall a conversation with the CEO of one of Europe's largest DIY groups. He was frustrated by the stuff that came across his desk and angry with himself for not prioritizing sensibly. I probed what was the basis for him prioritizing projects and proposals. It wasn't that clear. I suggested he put a plaque across his desk visible to both himself and his visitor. It would say: "Does this proposal add value for our customer?" I believe he did this and it helped – unfortunately, he moved on to new pastures shortly afterward. Here was a gimmicky and feeble attempt to capture the essential purpose of the organization and to force-fit it into the realities of the hierarchical pyramid.

Laloux has been able to tease out something really important when he talks of "evolutionary purpose." This is nothing to do with this kind of gimmick or a top-down consultation leading to a new inspirational mission statement! A DAD company becomes almost like a living organism, with a purpose of its own. If you can identify this evolutionary purpose, your company, like Buurtzorg, will have an essential purpose, which will unite and naturally inspire all stakeholders. It will not be necessary to paste it on your walls or your website, but it will breathe within the "soul" of your organization.

Pink and fuzzy claptrap? New-age rubbish? On the contrary, Laloux's deep study of the 12 companies found that, "Deep inside, everybody longs for work that serves a purpose in the world. Practices that put purpose at the heart of decision-making are likely to be embraced wholeheartedly, however unfamiliar they are at first."

One of the great achievements of Steve Jobs was to tease out and embody an "evolutionary purpose" at Apple. In his fascinating recent book, *Becoming Steve Jobs: How a Reckless Upstart Became a Visionary Leader*, Brent Schlender (Schlender, 2016), writing with Rick Tetzeli, describes a conversation shortly before he died between Jobs and the Apple design guru and close friend and confidante, Jony Ive. Ive recalled, "I remember a conversation in which we talked about how we define our metrics for feeling like we have really succeeded. We both agreed clearly it's not about share price. Is it about the number of computers we sell? No… it all came back to whether we felt really proud of what we had collectively designed and built." While Apple revolutionized computing and consumer electronics with superlative and innovative products, the metric that mattered was that consumers loved the product – its breakthrough capability and functional quality, yes, but also its look, feel and special design. The "evolutionary purpose" (although they did not call it that) was about bringing the full potential of the Digital Age to everyone with products that people love for their performance and beauty. "People do discern and value quality more than we give them credit for," Ive remembered. This focus on specialness around quality and the beauty of the product meant that all the other metrics – units sold, profitability, share price, earnings per share – were consequences of the focus, not measures of success in themselves.

The sense of purpose in your business needs to evolve, to be teased out. As in the case of Apple, it will, as its name implies, evolve and become evidence of the "soul" of your business. A platform like Loomio, widely applied across your organization, could be really helpful in getting there. You could also use established techniques such as appreciative inquiry in away-day sessions with groups of people. A useful starting trigger for reflection might be: "We change the world by…"

MILK THE FEEDBACK LOOP

The transformation process we have been exploring will be a journey – how long or complex, you can only guess at. My experiences with Storymaker show that getting started and sticking with it for at least six months is the key challenge. But almost immediately, there are important changes and signs of engagement. Create a space on your website or elsewhere, where experiences, good and bad, can be shared. Encourage your people to notice the difference. Encourage them to milk the feedback loop.

Make sure the board recognizes the changes and the benefits. After all, the leader's main role is to give the transformation oxygen to breathe and to avoid disruptive interferences from on high!

You can be confident that your new organization will be more agile and responsive to change. It will be leaner and flatter. Use of digital technologies will be widely adopted. You will be a magnet for the best talent. So the stakes are high.

CHAPTER 14

LEADERSHIP FOR A DISRUPTIVE WORLD

You may have noticed that throughout the earlier chapters, I have rarely written about "leaders" and "leadership." I have been talking about "senior executives," "top teams," "boards," "those in the executive suite." Why? Because real leadership is a rare and noble commodity, and there is unfortunately a chronic deficit in the kind of leaders needed for the migration toward survival, let alone success, in the disruptive world we have been exploring.

Let's face it, the probability is that without the right kind of leadership most incumbent enterprises in traditional industries, particularly consumer-facing industries, will fail to make the changes needed. Owners and boards need to understand that failure is the default setting – and many do. "Failure" may not mean bankruptcy, but it may mean a lingering decline.

The challenge is to identify what kind of leaders are needed. But where to find them?

ABOUT LEADERS

There are yards and yards of racks in offline and online bookstores dedicated to the topic of leadership. I am not going to add to their number. However, I think most of us would agree that we know a leader when we see one, and there is no standard psychometric nor behaviour profile.

We identify with leaders who listen, inform themselves, and then:

- Know where they are going
- Build a team dedicated to the cause
- Explain the challenge in inspirational, simple terms, however daunting
- Enrol the whole organization in facing the challenge and facing down obstacles
- Get "into the trenches with the foot-soldiers"
- Stick with it
- Distribute any spoils fairly.

Leadership is a state that is earned, not conferred from on high. Leaders are not to be confused with executives or managers. The last two terms are derived from the metaphor of the organization as machine – executives execute things that have been agreed upon; managers do things to influence others to do things that they, the managers, want.

Twice a year, I find myself in Burundi, Central Africa, where I provide business coaching to some of the most inspirational young leaders I know. They are committed to change their country from the ground up, by training young people in high-integrity leadership, challenging them to get involved in development projects in their communities, churches and civil society structures – this despite discouraging events taking place in their country, where their lives, and those of their families, may even be at risk.

During my last visit, we used Jim Collins' framework from his book, *Good to Great: Why Some Companies Make the Leap… and Others Don't* (Collins, 2001) as a basis for discussion. I explained that Collins had researched the characteristics that distinguished companies that consistently outperformed their industry peer groups – becoming "great" rather than just "good." I explained that in a classic concept of leadership, one might assume that the leaders behind these "great" companies are high profile, well known, charismatic "follow me" types. However, the study found the "good" to "great" leaders shared a common set of characteristics: they set up successors for success, they are extremely modest, and they have unwavering resolve. They cared and focused a lot more on the purposeful success of their companies, rather than on their own personal profile, success or reward. However, "great" leaders also show ferocious resolve – an almost stoic determination to do whatever needs to be done to make the company "great." Rather than taking credit for success, they give credit where it is due. Exceptional, consistent financial returns were consequences of doing things right (caring for customers, respecting suppliers), rather than objectives in their own right.

My Burundian coachees chose Nelson Mandela and Martin Luther King Jr. as their avatars for this kind of leader. We contrasted and compared their avatars with the "African Big Man" leadership style, which is so prevalent in their culture. The Big Man centralizes power, dispenses patronage, does not tolerate dissent, embodies the enterprise, and reaps a disproportionate share of the spoils. If they are to survive, employees in that environment must espouse the values, anticipate the needs, and play the game by the Big Man's rules.

Reflecting on this session and on the individual coaching sessions that followed, I noted in passing that I had experienced the Big Man leadership style in international enterprises! However, I found myself paying homage to Collins' "great" leaders – after all, if they were able to display this kind of leadership over many years while subjected to the obstacles of working within the constraints of a public enterprise (the stuckness predicament described in chapter 8), then they must be really special. How had the boards and remuneration committees found these people? And stuck with them?

In moving beyond denial, and surviving in a disruptive world, whatever posture companies end up adopting (as outlined in previous chapters), survivors will need leaders who chime with the times and the new realities. I reflected that most of the Burundian leaders I had been working with showed a kind of leadership which the millennials and post-millennials (chapter 3) would engage with. They were (perhaps surprisingly) technology-savvy people, with a leadership profile close to what the new world will require.

Collins' "great" companies had consistently outperformed their peers during an era of relative growth and stability, despite some ups and downs in different cycles. In the disruptive 4th Industrial Revolution world, things will be different.

The right leader and leadership is the single greatest determinant of success for survival and success in the disruptive world and for undertaking the changes needed. So it should be the number-one priority. Hiring and retaining the right talent within transformation programmes comes a close second. And remember, as we explored in chapter 7, the phenomenon of the inbreeding syndrome is such that growing the right leader for the disruptive age naturally from within may be difficult if not impossible.

So what does the leadership (owner, board and CEO) need to look like?

THE LEADER AS "MANAGER OF PARADOXES"

Our successful leaders will be comfortable with the ambiguities and apparent complexities of the disruptive world – particularly how to live with apparent problems of the old world, while preparing for the new. They will not ruminate like the mythical yokel: "If I was going there, guv'nor, I wouldn't start from here!"

As we discovered earlier, senior executives are usually formed from much the same mould – similar education, career progression and training. They are trained to look at the fundamental task of work as "problems to be solved."

My friend, David Mullins, has made a study of "failure." Many years ago, when he was right in the middle of his PhD thesis, he discovered that a fundamental plank of his research was wrong. His whole thesis seemed doomed to failure. David took time out to better understand the dynamics of "failure," and he met up with many learned academics in the sciences, philosophy, psychiatry and sociology.

He got to know Dr Barry Johnson, who had made a study of paradoxes or polarities. In his book, *Polarity Management: Identifying and Managing Unsolvable Problems* (Johnson, 2014), Johnson showed that some complex problems simply do not have "solutions." The key to being an effective leader is being able to recognize and manage such problems. He proposed a way of thinking and a set of principles that challenge you to look at situations in new ways. By recognizing and fully understanding the polarities of the problems you manage, you learn to set priorities and make a positive impact without being paralyzed by the often-unrealistic goal of formulating a total solution.

This work showed that, in a volatile world, successful transformational leaders are comfortable with ambiguity. They must see the handling of difficulties less in terms of "problems to be solved," and more as "paradoxes to be managed." While problems are finite, with a beginning and an end, which can be solved and where alternatives are mutually exclusive, paradoxes are infinite – alternatives can be mutually inclusive and can and must interact with each other. Paradoxes must be managed, not solved. Successful leaders must be bimodal in mindset – handling the new and the old in symbiosis.

The dynamics of failure, and therefore of the management of paradoxes, can be presented as an ellipse. Let us take the example of a large enterprise we have been working with that has acknowledged the existential need to become digital. A clear vision was agreed to at the highest levels. They were committed to moving from an undesirable "as is" state (a strong brand being disrupted by new business models) to a desired "future state" (a slimmed down, strong, digitally-enabled survivor). The company acknowledged the consequences of remaining in its traditional business model and resolved to migrate to the desired future state. Projects were defined, programmes were funded, resources were allocated, and expectations were raised. Some progress was made, but unintended consequences of the move become apparent – distraction of key people, mission creep, cost overruns, delays, impatience, and reputations were on the line – and this was impacting performance and results. What happened? The organization felt forced to reprioritize back to its original state – this was where calmer waters lay, where short-term fixes could produce results. They had travelled down the route of the ellipse and ended up where they started.

As "problem fixers," we see this example as failure. After all, the problem has not been solved, progress is slow and the existential threat remains. What is really going on here, and in the majority of similar cases? There is a chronic deficit of leadership of the kind required for a disruptive world – leaders who embrace paradoxes and are comfortable with ambiguity – and who are present in all levels of the enterprise (owners, boards and CEOs). A "paradox manager" leadership would have approached the difficulty differently, embracing the old and the new in parallel, and inspiring people to embrace the realities and expectations of the paradox.

THE LEADER FOCUSES ON OUTCOME

You notice I write outcome, not vision. In the previous chapter, we talked about Laloux's finding that the successful Digital Age Disruptive companies he researched were able to define an "evolutionary purpose" – a higher-level reason for being, which once teased out becomes like a living organism with a purpose of its own. David Mullins emphasizes that the fundamental role of the leadership in an organization facing transformation is to define and focus on a "higher-purpose question" than the challenge or difficulty being confronted. Our leader is able to engender a sense of shared identity, even love, for the company and a sense of working for a "greater cause." Interviewed by Brent Schendler for the book, *Becoming Steve Jobs*, Tim Cook, Jobs' successor as CEO, talked about Apple employees working for a greater cause: "Steve wanted people to love Apple… not just work for Apple, but really love Apple, and really understand at a deep level what Apple was about, about the values of the company. He didn't write them on the walls and make posters of them anymore, but he wanted people to understand them. He wanted people to work for a greater cause." In other words, the "higher-purpose question."

The leader's role is to tease out such a higher purpose outcome from within – he or she does not hire consultants to define it, nor impose it from on high. Nor is "survival" a sufficient, inspiring, higher-level outcome!

On its website, Google describes its mission: "To organize the world's information and make it universally accessible and useful" (Google, 2016). Internally, however, Google employees think about outcomes – for example, a power grid, smart homes, high-performance personal computing devices, robots, electric cars and other transportation, all linked together by "learning machines" customized to each organization, business or individual user. Worth getting out of bed for!

The big daddy of the leader who focuses on outcome has got to be Elon Musk. Here is someone who invested nearly all the proceeds he received from the disposal of PayPal into a truly global, galactic evolutionary purpose for all his ventures – to offer humanity a sustainable future! Love him or hate him (and many do!), this higher purpose drags the people around him forward toward dreams that "normal" people might consider impossible fantasies. In Ashlee Vance's fascinating biography, *Elon Musk: How the Billionaire CEO of SpaceX and Tesla Is Shaping our Future* (Vance, 2015), Musk describes his vision of the colonizing of Mars by rendering the surface inhabitable by humans as follows: "I would like to die thinking that humanity has a bright future. If we can solve sustainable energy and be well on our way to becoming a multiplanetary species with a self-sustaining civilization on another planet – to cope with the worst-case scenario happening and extinguishing consciousness, then... I think that would be really good." Wow! And people are waking up to the reality that, remarkably, Musk and his companies are delivering the building blocks of the dream. SpaceX has already disrupted the established business model for space transport by successfully delivering a supply capsule to the International Space Station at a fraction of the traditional cost. And in April 2016, SpaceX went further – its Falcon 9 successfully completed a soft landing on a barge offshore in the Atlantic Ocean, introducing the reality of recoverable propulsion rockets and potentially revolutionizing the economics of payload delivery to the Space Station and interplanetary travel. Another Musk company, SolarCity, is revolutionizing the provision of affordable solar power for homeowners. The Tesla Model 3 electric car is a huge hit just a few months after its recent launch, with nearly 400,000 cars already ordered. A truly beautiful electric car with free recharging points on offer fuelled by solar energy, the Tesla offers a realistic prospect to save the world from global warming and its addiction to carbon, putting flutters into the heart of Big Car.

The outcome that leaders of established enterprises in traditional industries focus on, the company's evolutionary purpose, may not be as ambitious as that of Elon Musk. But it will be ambitious and inspirational to employees and other stakeholders. Once defined, the outcome enters into the "soul" of the company, the reason for being. It becomes the point of reference for the leader at every moment, and for all the work of the enterprise.

THE LEADER BUILDS A STRONG TEAM, BUT DOES NOT COMPROMISE

In previous chapters, we have explored the things that should be done to build a Digital Age Disruptive enterprise – and the trends for replacement of jobs, including middle-management jobs, by machine and automation. While this process may shrink the enterprise more or less naturally, the strong may go as well as the weak. Our leaders build a team that "gets it" and is truly supportive. They do not shirk from difficult personnel decisions.

Our leader embraces the paradox of working with the people legacy and establishing the new. As discussed earlier, people at the top usually quickly buy into the outcome and the journey, and the same tends to be true for those at the "coal face" and the younger staff. The problem tends to lie within the middle layers of an organization and in the 45+ age group. But everyone is an individual. Robert Townsend made an impression on me way back in the 1970s when he described in his book, *Up the Organization* (Townsend, 1970), how he was consistently surprised about how the most unexpected employees stepped up to the plate once they were trusted, given responsibility and were treated as partners in an exciting enterprise. I have found the same.

Nevertheless, our leader conducts a people triage process calmly and fairly but, if necessary, ruthlessly. Those who have the required skill sets and step up to the plate in their behaviours become part of the team. Everyone gets a chance to be part of the team. But those who are actively obstructive or undermining are not tolerated. "Join the adventure, or leave," becomes the mantra. After England's rugby World Cup win in 2003, the coach, Clive Woodward, was quizzed on team selection, and particularly on high-profile players he had left out. He explained that some players are "energy sappers" in their behaviours both on and off the pitch, not only for the coach, but for their fellow players, and that their negative impact could be enormous. Our leader cannot afford to have "energy sappers" on the team. Netflix CEO Reed Hastings put it more succinctly – "Do not tolerate brilliant jerks."

When Steve Jobs picked up the reins again at Apple as CEO in 1998, the company was in a real mess. Still unproven as a transformative leader, Jobs focused immediately on right-sizing the company on the basis of the excellence of the people. In his book, *Becoming Steve Jobs*, Brett Schlender (Schlender, 2016) quotes Jobs: "When I returned to Apple, I was blown away by the fact that a third of the people there were A to A+ people – the kind you'd do anything to hire. Despite Apple's problems, they'd stayed, which was the miracle. That was the good karma of Apple. Another third were very good – you know, the really solid kind of people every company needs. And then there was another third who were unfortunate. I don't know whether they had ever been good or not, but it was time for them to leave. Unfortunately, a lot of these people were in management. Not only were they not doing the right things, but they were instructing everybody else to do the wrong things, too." This preparedness to be ruthless but fair and generous (as Apple was to those it let go) is critical. Notice that this is as much about attitude as star quality. And it is not about respecting slots in the organizational chart. This can be recast in light of the key people remaining. Sacrilege!

LEADERS MODEL AND TEACH PRODUCTIVE COLLABORATION

Leaders adopt many of the practices of Laloux's sample companies as possible, as summarized in chapter 13. They practice co-leadership principles and tools, for example, as described by Storymaker. They practice and encourage the practice of listening and productive collaboration. As far as possible, decision-making is fully participative, using platforms such as Loomio, to arrive at decisions that work for everyone.

THE LEADER SHOWS RESPECT AND CONSIDERATION

Deep in a consulting project with impossible work scope and deadlines (not uncommon in that profession), I was confronted back in the 1980s by a demand for a business dinner with the client, which clashed with a family birthday. My reflex was to prepare my excuses for the family, but I happened to mention this to my boss, Harland Riker, the then-president of Arthur D. Little in Europe. He told me he applied an unwavering principle – if there was a family commitment in the diary, this took precedence over all later demands, and that if this was explained to the client, nine times out of ten this was respected. "If they don't," he said, "we don't really want them for a client, do we?" I remember him saying, "Why should I show less respect to my family than to my business contacts?" I have tried to apply this behaviour and found that doing so has reaped its rewards – curiously by showing respect and consideration in this way, you gain as much if not more in return.

So our leader shows similar authentic respect for colleagues and business partners. I was much struck by the reference by Mark Greene and Catherine Butcher in their booklet, *The Servant Queen*, prepared as a commemoration of the 90th birthday of Queen Elizabeth II, which captures the kind of authentic respect a true leader can show: "This deep respect for others manifests itself in how she treats her staff – they are never 'servants' to her – and she almost never calls any of her staff when they are off-duty in the evenings, on the weekend or on holiday. She respects their privacy and their family life. Compare the Queen with the endless list of despotic rulers that litter history, or the many over-demanding bosses that sour our workplaces. By contrast, Elizabeth II shows us how power can be used considerately."

How does this gel with the uncompromising demand of successful entrepreneurs like Elon Musk and Steve Jobs, who demanded 12-hour days 7 days per week from employees to meet impossible deadlines, I hear you ask? And got rid of people who did not toe the line? Our leader will know that if people in the organization love their jobs and are treated considerately, they will work the hours necessary to be fulfilled without needing a climate of fear to perform.

THE LEADER AS COMMUNICATOR

Our leader of the remodelled company for the disruptive age will need to be an exceptional communicator – inside the company, and outside. In all media: electronic (embracing social media, blogs and podcasts), written, spoken, set piece and one-to-one, by voice and body language. Being a good communicator does not necessarily imply an extroverted, charismatic figure – as Jim Collins showed, the "great" communicators are often quiet, sincere types, accessible to all they come in contact with.

The task of remodelling the company will be huge – much like warfare. After all, for many companies, transformation will be an existential battle. Our leader will break down hierarchies and be in the trenches with the troops – the practitioners who design and build your products and services are in contact with customers and suppliers, who know competition intimately and who have the insight and knowledge of potential innovators. General Julian Thompson, the commander of the Royal Marine Commandos and the Parachute Regiment battalions during the recapture of the Falkland Islands by the British in 1982, kindly came to dinner with a few colleagues and business guests a few years ago and modestly shared his experiences. A renowned military historian and author, he recorded his experiences in his highly readable book, *No Picnic* (Thompson, 2008). What struck me most from that evening together was the fact that during the heat of the battle, Thompson was on the front line communicating directly with his commanders – not only because radio communications had broken down, but because this was the way to ensure clarity of what was needed – both in words and in demeanour, transmitting the calm certainty that inspires exceptional performance.

This is the kind of communication that our leaders will need. They will spend little time in the ivory tower. Much of the "stuff" of managerialistic organizational practice, masquerading as communication, will be discouraged – meetings, PowerPoint presentations, and so on. It is striking to read how much time Steve Jobs, as CEO of one of the most successful corporations in history, spent in one-to-one contact with the key people in his organization – not only at the top, but in the design studios and at the workbenches. A similar, almost obsessive hands-on style was adopted by Elon Musk at Tesla and SpaceX.

OUR LEADERS WILL BE PAID WELL, BUT NOT EXCESSIVELY

Yes, our leaders will be very well rewarded, but without the excesses that can so wind up employees and the general public alike. They will be motivated more by "changing the world (or at least the enterprise!)" than by money. They will be driven by the higher purpose of the enterprise.

I was talking, not long back, to a group of recent graduates from top European schools and asking what kind of enterprises they wanted to join. Many wanted to start in investment banking or consulting as a way-station to starting a disruptive business. Some were, of course, highly motivated by the acquisition of wealth, but they were in the minority. I challenged them on why they did not want to make a difference by joining an established enterprise and helping to make it fit for purpose in the disruptive world. One said: "You just don't get it, David. We hate those greedy b_____!" And there was much nodding in the rest of the group.

Face it, executive pay is an issue, and if you are to attract the best new talent, you must create a culture where greed is not present. Our leader must embody this.

When Mark Carney, the governor of the Bank of England, was talking about the "Tragedy of Horizons" in his speech to the insurers at Lloyd's of London in September 2015, he was talking specifically about climate change as it related to insurers' preparedness to deal with a new category of risk. He defined the "Tragedy of Horizons" as the chronic inability of business and political leaders to tackle challenges beyond their short-term horizon. "It presents an existential threat to the status quo, yet hardly figures in day-to-day operational planning. It's too big, too scary and, most of all, too distant to start planning for."

The "Tragedy of Horizons" can be applied to other great issues of our time: unsustainable population growth leading to depletion of the earth's resources, migration and multiculturalism, and inequality. However, executive pay is definitely an under-the-horizon issue that company boards need to take seriously now.

"Bankers' bonuses" has become shorthand for stigmatizing inequality in remuneration, which survivors in a disruptive world are going to need to get their arms around. It is also a symbol for many for all that is wrong with an unbridled shareholder capitalistic system. It is not just members of the Occupy Movement or "Disgusted from Tunbridge Wells" in the letter pages who reject the scale of inequality that is so widespread in Western enterprises, particularly in the US and UK. Ordinary members of Generation X and millennials see executive pay (both the scale and the inequalities implicit in it) as a reason for "rejecting how the world does business." How can the kind of leader I have been describing be credible as a partner to employees in disruptive innovation and survival if he or she receives 130 times as much as the average employee? Yes, average, not lowest paid! This was the ratio calculated recently by a think tank, the High Pay Centre, applying to the 100 companies listed on the UK's FTSE exchange.

The issue of excessive executive pay is potentially dangerous. If regulation and self-regulation do not kick in effectively soon, a social and political turmoil may well result sooner than we might think.

Levels of executive pay have become out of kilter with what is needed for a successful lifestyle, let alone with the notion of equality that most people would recognize. Sadly, the primary measure of many business people's success and self-worth is accumulation of wealth. Not adequate wealth to live comfortably, to look after my retirement and to give a good start in life to my family, but ever more wealth, just for the sake of it. This is how some people keep score of their own self-worth! Sad, but true.

I cannot remember the number of times social conversations with senior executives have centred around meeting bonus targets, pension expectations on retirement, smart but legal ways to reduce taxes, or extravagances in lifestyle and consumption. Of course, I acknowledge that people who have accumulated wealth can, and do, do positive things with it in philanthropy and the arts, for example, and that not everyone is like this to the same degree.

The "great" leaders for the 4ᵗʰ Industrial Revolution, who guide established enterprises through disruptive change, will measure self-worth on a broader palette. These people cannot be "incentivized" in classic, purely financial ways, indeed the very concept of incentivization is part of the metaphor of the machine, and is in danger of skewing the way they go about their jobs. So remuneration committees will need to think about more acceptable and imaginative ways of structuring senior leaders' remuneration. This is not just about reduction in overall levels, although there is clearly some kind of market failure going on if such high levels of pay exist. It is more about the philosophy of pay and it how it can meet the needs both of the leaders and the ideals they espouse.

UNEARTHING THE LEADER

Where do you find such people?

Perhaps they might already be in your organization? After all, your own people will be better placed than outsiders to appreciate the nature of the challenge the company faces. When did you last commission a search from a specialist recruiter *within* your company?

The leaders may be people who have launched, developed and exited from a successful disruptive business. They are already wealthy, but bored. They want to make a difference, perhaps to the industry they have contributed to disrupting. They have experienced the culture and practices of a Digital Age disruptive organization, but understand the realities of the established order. They are disruptors, but not mavericks.

If the right leader cannot be found within the company, a search must surely extend beyond the graduate/MBA population – leaders of social enterprises, head teachers, public health administrators, civil service, the military. Performance directors of team sports or artistic directors in the arts appear to have many of the characteristics we have been talking about.

POSTSCRIPT: SUMMARY AND FINAL THOUGHTS

POSTSCRIPT: SUMMARY AND FINAL THOUGHTS

It seems right to have closed this inquiry into denial in the face of obvious and immediate disruptive forces with leadership.

We need to remember that leaders are only human and that there are limits to what one man or woman can do to in the face of overwhelming disruptive forces. We only have to look at the stuckness predicament of our world leaders in the face of day-to-day realities to see this. Do they not seem powerless in the face of disruptive forces battling economic meltdown, terrorism, war and forced migration, let alone the "over the horizon" issues of population growth, climate change and nuclear proliferation? Where are the real leaders, people ask. We need another Churchill, they say!

Perhaps the reality is that leaders can have little impact beyond building awareness and galvanizing friends and colleagues to face realities and deal with the consequences. As in its earlier stages, the 4th Industrial Revolution will be messy. To go back to the metaphor of an earlier age, do not continue forging horseshoes, think of making bicycles and wrought-iron gates!

I promised my readers that this book would not be a treatise on despair, but one offering hope. I hope you will have acquired a better insight into the nature of disruption affecting you and that you have a framework to better plan for your futures, both personal and in the workplace. After all, we are all leaders – we can build awareness and galvanize our friends and colleagues to accept realities, and to take charge of our world.

Let me remind you of the main messages of the book.

Disruptive forces are already fundamentally changing the traditional landscape of business and the process will accelerate rapidly (part 1).

- Digital disruptors, both established and new, are a breed of competitors that will threaten your established business model and value networks with suppliers and customers, perhaps fatally.
- Big Data, the algorithms for exploiting them, artificial intelligence and robots will revolutionize the way you do business and the model of the enterprise.
- New generational tribes of consumers (millennials and post-millennials) think and behave fundamentally differently from what you are used to and the way they interact with technology means a fundamental reappraisal of your approach to customers.

199

- Your business model, including IT infrastructure and systems, will no longer be fit for purpose in an increasingly "platformed" world.
- The traditional organizational model you are using has reached its "sell-by date," and if you are to compete you must radically change it.

Denial of the scope, scale and reach of these disruptive changes is widespread; denial is the default setting of most executives within established enterprises (part 2).

- Denial is a natural response to threats of fundamental change, given how the brain works and the nature of established behaviours at work.
- Inbreeding at the top of organizations is widespread and there is little enrichment of the gene pool from outside; this reinforces denial.
- Executives find themselves trapped by the realities of the shareholder capital model; they are in a "stuckness predicament," unable to react to disruptive change.

Established enterprises in traditional industries can survive if they accept reality and take remedial action; but it will not be easy – if they do nothing, they will fail (part 3).

- Moving from a state of denial to acceptance is a vital first step; this means taking positive steps to gain understanding of the threats and opportunities, and acquiring a determination to "get cracking."
- Whatever else you do, you will need to take action to move progressively toward a business model with "platform" features, making the best of your legacy and making your business model compatible with platforms.
- Some enterprises could envisage a big move like Dell has done; this usually means escaping the constraints of the public enterprise by going private, with a private equity partner with deep pockets.
- You can and must adopt a "disrupt yourself" posture; there are lots of things you can do to encourage disruptive innovation and change your company from within.
- You need to take steps to become a Digital Age Disruptive organization, fit to inspire the new generations and to deal with the realities of the disruptive world.

- A new style of leadership will be critical for survival; acknowledging that this will be different and looking in non-traditional places for these leaders will be vital.

I very much hope that I have kick-started a conversation on this vital topic. I believe that encouraging enterprises to wake up to the reality of what is about to hit them is a great issue of our time. Established companies – with their histories, their workforces, their brands, their products and services, their capabilities of all kinds – can and surely must be able to co-exist after the 4th Industrial Revolution with the new Digital Age corporations. But there is no divine right that they will do so. Many, perhaps most, will not make the transition to sustainable survival. In fact, a comparison of the constituent companies in the Dow Jones Industrial Average, FTSE 100, CAC40, Nikkei 225 or other leading indexes on other exchanges today with 10 or 15 years ago already makes for sober reading. Darwinism is in action and is accelerating! As Stephen Warrington points out in the foreword to this book, the subject matter is critical. "It is for those on whom the lion's share of our economy and prosperity depends; those who lead, or aspire to lead, the organizations, large and small, that provide most of our products and services, and employ most of our people. Many of these organizations are at risk of becoming moribund."

I do hope you will join the conversation at www.disruptiondenial.com. Feel free to share your thoughts with me at david.guillebaud@disruptiondenial.com.

REFERENCES

Addiss, S. &. L. S., 1993. *Tao Te Ching by Lao Tzu*. Indianapolis: Hackett Publishing Inc..

Buurtzorg, 2016. *The History of Buurtzorg*. [Online]
Available at: http://buurtzorgusa.org/about.html [Accessed 12 February 2016]

Carney, M., 2015. *Breaking the tragedy of the horizon - climate change and financial stability - speech by Mark Carney*. [Online]
Available at: http://www.bankofengland.co.uk/publications/Pages/speeches/2015/844.aspx [Accessed 12 December 2015]

Choudary, S. P., 2015. *Platform Scale: How an emerging business model helps startups build large empires with minimum investment*. 1st ed. s.l.:Platform Thinking Labs Pte. Ltd.

Christensen, C. M., 1997. *Innovator's Dilemma: When New Technologies Cause Great Firms to Fail*. Boston: Harvard Business Review Press.

Collins, J., 2001. *Good To Great: Why Some Companies Make the Leap... and Others Don't*. 1st ed. s.l.:Random House.

Gartner, 2015. *Bimodal IT*. [Online]
Available at: http://www.gartner.com/it-glossary/bimodal [Accessed 3 January 2016]

Gill, M., 2014. *Digital Business Transformation Will Gain Critical Mass In 2015*. [Online]
Available at: http://blogs.forrester.com/martin_gill/14-11-07-digital_business_transformation_will_gain_critical_mass_in_2015 [Accessed 10 December 2015]

Gladwell, M., 2006. *Blink: The Power of Thinking Without Thinking*. 1st ed. London: Penguin Books.

Google, 2016. *Google's mission is to organize the world's information and make it universally accessible and useful*. [Online]
Available at: https://www.google.com/about/company/ [Accessed 1 January 2016]

Haldane, A., 2015. *Labour's Share - speech by Andy Haldane*. [Online]
Available at: http://www.bankofengland.co.uk/publications/Pages/speeches/2015/864.aspx [Accessed 4 January 2016]

Hansson, D. H. &. F. J., 2010. *ReWork: Change the Way You Work Forever*. 1st ed. Chatham: Vermillion.

Heidrick & Struggles, 2015. *The CEO Report*, London: Heidrick & Struggles.

IBM, 2016. *Big Data at the Speed of Business.* [Online]
Available at: http://www-01.ibm.com/software/data/bigdata/library.html
[Accessed 5 February 2016]

IDC, 2014. *The Digital Universe of Opportunities.* [Online]
Available at: http://www.emc.com/leadership/digital-universe/2014iview/
executive-summary.htm [Accessed 15 December 2015]

Johnson, B., 2014. *Polarity Management: Identifying and Managing
Unsolvable Problems.* 1st ed. Amherst: HRD Press.

Laloux, F., 2014. *Reinventing Organizations: A Guide to Creating
Organizations Inspired by the Next Stage in Human Consciousness.* 1st ed.
Brussels: Nelson Parker.

Madsbjerg, C. &. R. M., 2014. *Moment of Clarity.* 1st ed. Boston:
Harvard Business Review press.

McAfee, A. &. B. E., 2012. *Big Data: The Management Revolution.*
[Online]
Available at: https://hbr.org/2012/10/big-data-the-management-
revolution/ar [Accessed 12 December 2015]

McQuivey, J., 2013. *Digital Disruption: Unleashing the Next Wave of
Innovation.* Las Vegas: Amazon Publishing.

Nassos Stylianou, T. N. G. F. A. F. R. B. a. J. W., 2015. *Will a robot take
your job?* [Online]
Available at: http://www.bbc.co.uk/news/technology-34066941 [Accessed
7 January 2016]

OpenLegacy, 2016. *OpenLegacy Server.* [Online]
Available at: http://openlegacy.com/openlegacy-server/ [Accessed 15
December 2015]

Peterson, H., 2014. *Millennials Are Old News – Here's Everything You
Should Know About Generation Z.* [Online]
Available at: http://www.businessinsider.com/generation-z-spending-
habits-2014-6?IR=T [Accessed 3 January 2016]

PewResearchCenter, 2010. *Milennials: A Portrait of Generation Next,* s.l.:
Pew Research Center.

Porter, M. E., 1980. *Competitive Strategy: Techniques for Analyzing
Industries and Competitors.* 1st ed. New York: The Free Press.

Prodhan, G., 2015. *Global industrial robot sales rose 27 pct in 2014.* [Online]

Available at: http://www.reuters.com/article/industry-robots-sales-idUSL6N0WM1NS20150322 [Accessed 4 January 2016]

Regalado, A., 2014. *Is Google Cornering the Market on Deep Learning?*. [Online]
Available at: https://www.technologyreview.com/s/524026/is-google-cornering-the-market-on-deep-learning/ [Accessed 2 January 2016]

Robertson, B. J., 2015. *Holacracy: The New Management System for a Rapidly Changing World.* 1st ed. s.l.:Henry Holt and Company.

Russell Reynolds, 2015. *Productive Disruptors: Five Characteristics That Differentiate Transformational Leaders.* [Online]
Available at: http://www.russellreynolds.com/insights/thought-leadership/productive-disruptors-five-characteristics-that-differentiate-transformational-leaders [Accessed 14 December 2015]

Savage, R., 2015. *There are more foreigners than Oxbridge grads at the top of FTSE 100 companies.* [Online]
Available at: http://www.managementtoday.co.uk/news/1367322/there-foreigners-oxbridge-grads-top-ftse-100-companies/ [Accessed 5 November 2015]

Schaal, D., 2015. *Interview: Accor Hotels CEO on Moving Fast While Others Fail.* [Online]
Available at: http://skift.com/2015/11/19/interview-accor-hotels-ceo-on-moving-fast-while-others-fail/ [Accessed 20 November 2015]

Schlender, B., 2016. *Becoming Steve Jobs: The evolution of a reckless upstart into a visionary leader.* s.l.:Sceptre.

Schumpeter, J., 1942. *Capitalism, Socialism, and Democracy.* First ed. s.l.:Harper & Brothers.

Sloan, A. P., 1964. *My years with General Motors.* 1st ed. s.l.:Doubleday.

Solomon, M., 2015. *2016 Is The Year Of The Millennial Customer: Is Your Customer Experience Ready?* [Online]
Available at: http://www.forbes.com/sites/micahsolomon/2015/11/14/2016-is-the-year-of-the-millennial-customer-heres-how-to-be-ready/#5d9afad26e72 [Accessed 15 January 2016]

Stolzenberg, G., 1978. *Psychology and Biology of Language and Thought: Essays in Honour of Eric Lenneberg.* s.l.:Academic Press.

Taptiklis, T., 2007. *Unmanaging: Opening up the Organization to its Own Unspoken Knowledge.* 1st ed. New York: Palgrave Macmillan.

Daily Telegraph, T., 2015. *Professor John Hunt - obituary.* [Online]
Available at: http://www.telegraph.co.uk/news/obituaries/11968616/
Professor-John-Hunt-obituary.html [Accessed 14 February 2016]

The Hunt. 2015. [Film] Directed by Alastair Fothergill. UK: Silverback
Films; BBC.

Daily Telegraph, 2015. *Jim Slater, financier - obituary.* [Online]
Available at: http://www.telegraph.co.uk/news/obituaries/12006338/Jim-
Slater-financier-obituary.html [Accessed 21 November 2015]

Thompson, J., 2008. 3 *Commando Brigade in the Falklands: No Picnic.*
s.l.:Pen & Sword Military.

Townsend, R. L., 1970. *Up the Organization: How to Stop the Corporation
from Stifling People and Strangling Profits.* 1st ed. s.l.:Knopf.

Vance, A., 2015. *Elon Musk: How the Billionaire CEO of SpaceX and Tesla
is Shaping our Future.* s.l.:Virgin Books.

Zega, R., 2015. *Bank of America Picks 10 Key Stocks to Watch as Robots
Take Over the World.* [Online]
Available at: http://www.bloomberg.com/news/articles/2015-11-05/bofa-
picks-10-key-stocks-to-watch-as-robots-take-over-the-world [Accessed 3
January 2016]

AN INTRODUCTION TO

DAVID GUILLEBAUD

David Guillebaud advises CEOs and top management teams on strategy and transformation issues, especially on digital disruption. He challenges executive teams to seriously address the scope, scale, reach and pace of disruptive change, particularly from digital technologies. David's rich mix of business experience gives him empathy to the predicament in which large, established enterprises find themselves.

He had a wide-ranging early career on the fast track with Esso Petroleum in the UK, including a stint in the executive suite.

After starting his career in the oil industry, David gained his MBA from INSEAD, and then joined Arthur D. Little where he became leader of its worldwide travel, tourism and hospitality practice. From the early 1990s, he was already providing digital transformation and strategic advice to top teams from airlines, hotel groups, cruise lines and travel companies. He remains a well-known figure in these industries.

David was director of a niche investment bank in London in the late 1980s and managing director of its advisory arm, during which time he advised on cross-border strategies in Europe. He has also experienced the ups and downs of being an entrepreneur: he was a leader in three start-ups – a consulting firm later sold to a large American group, a travel software company successfully sold to a cable company, and a dot-com travel business that ran out of money! He continues to invest in interesting companies as a business angel.

As chairman of several companies, mainly privately owned, David has had direct experience dealing with disruptive change. For example, he oversaw the wind-down of significant enterprises – one in Germany and one with activities across Europe.

These days, David works part time as an associate partner at Elixirr, a fast-growing, London-based consulting firm with a strong digital technology and IT heritage. Elixirr is itself disrupting the consulting industry with its entrepreneurial involvement with both start-ups and traditional enterprises, "responding to tomorrow's disruption today." David linked up with Elixirr after several years in the role of chairman of the international operations of Diamond Management and Technology Partners in London and after a spell with PwC as a senior adviser following its acquisition of Diamond.

With a strong interest in Africa and economic development, David is chairman of Great Lakes Outreach, which works with Christian leaders in the Great Lakes region of Central Africa. He lives in France.